Dorothea Brande's Wake Up and Live Collection

**Containing "Wake Up and Live!"
and "Becoming a Writer"**

by Dorothea Brande

Edited and with Forward by **Dr. Robert C. Worstell**

**Visit <u>Midwest Journal Press</u> for more material and
related books.**

<u>http://dorotheabrandewakeupandlive.midwestjournalpress.com</u>

Cover photo credit: "african fi"

CW01496309

Table of Contents

Forward

What could you accomplish if you knew for a fact that you would succeed at <u>anything</u> you set out to do?

This is the formula which Dorothea Brande discovered for herself, and applying it changed her life from one where she considered herself to be a personal failure into one of being a noted success.

Her book, "Becoming A Writer" is still in print today, and is held as a cornerstone book for beginning authors to absorb while they master the disciplines of writing fiction – or anything else. And her experiences in teaching a class of fiction writers was "grist for the mill" as she studied success itself.

I ran into Brande's "Wake Up and Live!" when tracing the influence of Napoleon Hill's "Think and Grow Rich". Earl Nightingale found a copy of Hill's book and went on to yet another success, crediting Hill for the positive influence. In Nightingale's subsequent Gold recording "The Strangest Secret", he mentions "Wake Up and Live" as a key book to study.

And is it ever a study for anyone and everyone... While it reads well (she is an exceptional writer) it also simply brings the basics of affirmation and self-esteem training to the forefront. It's easy to follow and not didactic – but is based on serious studies into how people tick and what motivates them to either succeed or fail in their life-journey.

This collection shows the real-world application of what Brande had uncovered that fateful day. It shows how she applied her single motto, "**Act As If It Were Impossible to Fail**" to her own life.

And thousands, if not millions of budding writers have her to thank for it.

Being able to study these two books in one volume gives all of us the chance to improve our lives immeasurably from here on out.

Again, if you want to get all the key tools for self-improvement – get the books Nightingale recommended. You'll find links in the Resource section below.

Good Hunting – and Best of Luck!

Robert C. Worstell

Wake Up and Live!

Introduction

TWO YEARS ago I came across a formula for success which has revolutionized my life. It was so simple, and so obvious once I had seen it, that I could hardly believe it was responsible for the magical results which followed my putting it into practice.

The first thing to confess is that two years ago I was a failure. Oh, nobody knew it except me and those who knew me well enough to see that I was not doing a tenth of what could be expected of me. I held an interesting position, lived not too dull a life---yet there was no doubt in my own mind, at least, that I had failed. What I was doing was a substitute activity for what I had planned to do; and no matter how ingenious and neat the theories were which I presented to myself to account for my lack of success, I knew very well that there was more work that I should be doing, and better work, and work more demonstrably my own.

Of course I was always looking for a way out of my impasse. But when I actually had the good fortune to find it, I hardly believed in my own luck. At first I did not try to analyze or explain it. For one thing, the effects of using the formula were so remarkable that I was almost on the verge of being superstitious about the matter; it seemed like magic, and it doesn't do to inquire too closely into the reasons for a spell or incantation! More realistic than that, there was---at that time--- still a trace of wariness about my attitude. I had tried to get out of my difficulties many times before, had often seemed to be about to do so, and then had found them closing in around me again as relentlessly as ever. But the main reason for my taking so little time to analyze or explain the effects of the formula after I once began to use it consistently was that I was much too busy and having far too much fun.

It was enough to revel in the ease with which I did work hitherto impossible for me, to see barriers I had thought impenetrable melt away, to feel the inertia and timidity which had bound me for years dropping off like unlocked fetters.

For I had been years in my deadlock; I had known what I wanted to do, had equipped myself for my profession---and got nowhere. Yet I had chosen my life work, which was writing, early, and had started out with high hopes. Most of the work I had finished had met a friendly reception. But then when I tried to take the next step and go onto a more mature phase it was as though I had been turned to stone. I felt as if I could not start.

Of course it goes without saying that I was unhappy. Not miserably and painfully unhappy, but just nagged at and depressed by my own ineffectuality. I busied myself at editing, since I seemed doomed to fail at the more creative side of literature; and I never ceased harrying myself, consulting teachers and analysts and psychologists and physicians for advice as to how to get out of my pit. I read and inquired and thought and worried; I tried every suggestion for relief. Nothing worked more than temporarily. For a while I might engage in feverish activity, but never for more than a week or two. Then the period of action would suddenly end, leaving me as far from my goal as ever, and each time more deeply discouraged.

Then, between one minute and the next, I found the idea which set me free. This time I was not consciously looking for it; I was engaged on a piece of research in quite another field. But I came across a sentence in the book I was reading. HUMAN PERSONALITY, by F. W. H. Myers, which was so illuminating that I put the book aside to consider all the ideas suggested in that one penetrating hypothesis. When I picked up the book again I was a different person.

Every aspect, attitude, relation of my life was altered. At first, as I say, I did not realize that. I only knew, with increasing certainty from day to day, that at last I had found a talisman for counteracting failure and inertia and discouragement and that it worked. That was quite enough for me! My hands and my days were so full that there was no time for introspection. I did sometimes drop off to sleep, after doing in a short while what once would have seemed to me a gigantic task, thinking, like the old lady of the nursery rhyme, "This is none of I!" But "I" was reaping the rewards, beyond doubt: the books I had wanted to write for so long and had so agonizingly failed to write were flowing, now, as fast as the words would go on paper, and so far from feeling drained by the activity, I was continually finding new ideas which had been hidden, as it were, behind the work that had "backed up" in my mind and made a barrier.

Here is the total amount of writing I was able to do in the twenty years before I found my formula---the little writing which I was painfully, laboriously, protestingly able to do. For safety's sake I have over-estimated the items in each classification, so a generous estimate of it comes to this: Seventeen short stories, twenty book-reviews, half a dozen newspaper items, one attempt at a novel, abandoned less than a third of the way through. An average of less than two completed pieces of work per year! For the two years after my moment of illumination, this is the record: Three books (the first two in just two weeks less than the first year, and both successful in their different fields), twenty-four articles, four short stories, seventy-two lectures, the scaffolding of three more books; and innumerable letters of consultation and professional advice sent to all parts of the country.

Nor are those by any means the only results of applying my formula. As soon as I discovered how it worked in the one matter of releasing my energy for writing, I began to be curious as to what else it might do for me, and to try acting upon it in other fields where I had had trouble. The tentativeness and timidity which had crippled me in almost every aspect of my life dropped away. Interviews, lectures, engagements which I had driven myself to giving against the grain every minute, became pleasurable experiences. On the other hand, a dozen stupid little exploitations of myself which I had allowed--- almost in a penitential spirit---so long as I was in my deadlock were ended then and there. I was on good terms with myself at last, no longer punishing and exhorting and ruthlessly driving myself, and so no longer allowing myself to be unnecessarily bored and tired.

Although my formula had worked with such striking consequences for me, I told very few of my friends about it. In the almost fatuous egotism which I seem to share with ninety-nine percent of my fellows, I thought my case was unique: that no one had ever got into quite such a state of ineffectiveness before, nor would be able to apply the formula I used so successfully on their own difficulties.

From time to time, now that I was no longer living in such a state of siege as made me blind to all outside happenings, I did see indications here and there that another was wasting their life in much the same way that I had wasted mine; but I had had the good fortune to emerge and so, I thought, would they, in good time. Except for chance I would never have thought of publicly offering the simple program which had helped me so; I might, indeed, never have realized that to a greater or less extent most adults are living inadequate lives and suffering in consequence.

But some months ago I was asked to lecture to a group of booksellers, and the subject which was tentatively given me was "The Difficulties of Becoming a Writer." Now in my first book I had gone into those difficulties pretty thoroughly; I had no desire to read a chapter from an already published book to an audience the members of which were in a little better way to have read the chapter than almost any other group would have been. Beginning to prepare the lecture I could think of nothing further to add to the subject than to say frankly that the most difficult of all tasks for a writer was learning to counteract their own inertia and cowardice. So, fearing at first that my talk would have somewhat the sound of "testifying to grace" in an old- fashioned prayer-meeting, I began to consider the subject and prepare my speech.

The conclusions I came are in this book: that we are victims to a Will to Fail; that unless we see this in time and take action against it we die without accomplishing our intentions; that there is a way of counteracting that Will which gives results that seem like magic. I gave my lecture. What was really startling to me was to see how it was received. Until the notes, the letters, the telephone-calls began to come in, I had thought the report of how one person overcame a dilemma might interest many of the audience mildly and help two or three hearers who found themselves in somewhat the same plight.

But it seemed that my audience, almost to a man, was in the state I had described, that they all were looking for help to get out of it. I gave the lecture twice more; the results were the same. I was flooded with messages, questions, and requests for interviews.

Best of all were three reports which came to me within two weeks.

Three of my hearers had not waited for a fuller exposition, or taken it for granted that the formula would not work for them, but had put it into immediate practice. One had written and sold a story which had haunted her for years, but which had seemed too extraordinary to be likely to sell. A man had gone home and quietly ended the exploitation of himself by a temperamental sister, and had made arrangements to resume evening work in a line that he had abandoned at his sister's insistence; to his astonishment, his sister, once she thoroughly understood that he refused to be handicapped longer, had seemed to wake from a long period of peevish hypochondria and was happier than she had been in years. The third case was too long and too personal to recount here, but in many ways it was the best of them all. Well, there were three persons, at least, who found the formula efficacious; and, like me, each of them found something rather awe-inspiring about the results.

We all live so far below the possible level for our lives that when we are set free from the things which hamper us so that we merely approach the potentialities in ourselves, we seem to have been entirely transfigured. It is in comparison with the halting, tentative, hesitant lives we let ourselves live that the full, normal life that is ours by right seems to partake of the definitely super-normal. When that is seen, it is easy to discover that all men and women of effective lives, whether statesmen, philosophers, artists or men of business, use, sometimes entirely unconsciously, the same mental attitude in which to do their work that their less fortunate fellows must either find for themselves or die without discovering.

Occasionally, as the reading of biographies and autobiographies shows, enlightenment comes through religion, philosophy, or wholehearted admiration for another; and the individual, although often feeling still weak in himself, is sustained by his devotion, is often capable of feats of endurance, effectiveness or genius which cause us to marvel at him. But those who are not born with this knowledge of the way to induce the state in which successful work is done, who do not learn it so early that they cannot remember a time when they did not know it, or who for some reason cannot find in religion or philosophy the strength that they need to counteract their own ineffectiveness, can still teach themselves by conscious effort to get the best from their lives. As they do so, many other things which have puzzled them become clear.

But this book is not the history of the growth of an idea. It is intended to be a practical handbook for those who would like to escape from futility and begin to live happily and well.

Chapter 1 - Why Do We Fail?

WITH the time and energy we spend in making failure a certainty we might have certain success.

A nonsensical paradox? No; fortunately it is a sober, literal truth, one which holds a great deal of promise.

Suppose a man had an appointment a hundred miles north of his home, and that if he kept it he would be sure of having health, much happiness, fair prosperity, for the rest of his life. He has just time enough to get there, just enough gas in his car. He drives out, but decides that it would be more fun to go twenty-five miles south before starting out in earnest.

That is nonsense! Yes, isn't it? The gas had nothing to do with it; time had no preference as to how it would be spent; the road ran north as well as south, yet he missed his appointment. Now, if that man told us that, after all, he had quite enjoyed the drive in the wrong direction, that in some ways he found it pleasanter to drive with no objective than to try to keep a date, that he had had a touching glimpse of his old home by driving south, should we praise him for being properly philosophical about having lost his opportunity? No, we should think he had acted like an imbecile. Even if he had missed his appointment by getting into a daydream in which he drove automatically past a road sign or two, we should still not absolve him. Or if he had arrived too late from having lost his way when he might have looked up his route on a good map and failed to do so before starting, we might commiserate with him, but we should indict him for bad judgment.

Yet when it comes to going straight to the appointments we make with ourselves and our own fulfillment we all act very much like the hero of this silly fable: we drive the wrong way. We fail where we might have succeeded by spending the same power and time.

Failure indicates that energy has been poured into the wrong channel. It takes energy to fail.

Now this is something which we seldom see at once. Because we commonly think of failure as the conventional opposite of success, we continue to make false antitheses of the qualities which attend success and failure. Success is bracing, active, alert; so the typical attitude of failure, we believe, must be lethargy, inertia, a supine position.

True enough; but that does not mean that no energy is being used. Let any psychologist tell you how much energy a mature person must expend to resist motion.

A powerful struggle must be waged against the forces of life and movement in order to remain inert, although this struggle takes place so far beneath the surface of our lives that we do not always become aware of it. Physical inaction is no true sign that life-force is not being burned away. So even the idler is using fuel while they dream.

When failure comes about through devoting precious hours to time-killing pursuits, we can all see that energy is being diverted from its proper channel. But there are ways of killing time which do not look like dissipation. They can seem, on the contrary, like conscientious and dutiful hard work, they often draw praise and approval from onlookers, and arouse a sense of complacency in us. It is only by looking more closely, by discovering that this work gets us nowhere, that it both tires us and leaves us unsatisfied, that we see here again energy is being devoted to the pursuit of failure.

But why should this be so? Why, if, with the same energy we must use in any case, we might be succeeding, do we so seldom live the lives we hoped and planned to live? Why do we accomplish so little, and thwart ourselves senselessly? Why, when we start late, or run out of gas because of carelessness, or miss road-signs through daydreaming, do we think we are being properly philosophical when we give ourselves and others excuses for failure which will not hold water? No one truly consoles themselves by considering that a bird in the hand is worth two in the bush, that to travel hopefully is better than to arrive, that half-a-loaf is better than no bread. Such proverbs are the cynical distillation of experience, but they are nothing to live by. We deceive no one, although our compromises and excuses are accepted by our fellows as long as they are in the same boat. The successful man or woman listens to such whistling in the dark with amusement and incredulity, privately concluding that there is a great deal of hypocrisy loose in the world. They have the best of evidence that the rewards of well directed activity far surpass all the by-products of failure, that one infinitesimal accomplishment in reality is worth a mountain of dreams.

Even as we tell of the compensation of failure we are not quite comfortable. We do not truly believe---although our proverbs sound as though we did---that one must choose either success or the good life. We know that those who succeed see the same sunsets, breathe the same air, love and are loved no less than failures; and in addition they have something more: the knowledge that they have chosen to move in the direction of life and growth instead of acquiescing in death and decay. However we may talk, we know that Emerson was right when he wrote: "Success is constitutional; depends on a plus condition of mind and body, on power of work, on courage." Then why do we fail? Especially, why do we work hard at failure?

Because, beside being creatures subject to the Will to Live and the Will to Power, we are driven by another will, the Will to Fail, or die.

It is possible to get back the energy that is now going into failure and use it to healthy ends. There are certain facts--- plain, universal, psychological truths---which, when once seen, bring us to definite conclusions. From those conclusions we can make a formula on which to act. There is a simple, practical procedure which will turn us around and set our faces in the right direction. It is the formula, as we have said, on which, consciously or unconsciously, every successful person acts.

The procedure is simple, the first steps of putting it into practice so easy that those who prefer to dramatize their difficulties may refuse to believe that anything so uncomplicated could possibly help them. On the other hand, since it takes little time and soon brings its own evidence that, simple or not, its consequences are frequently amazing, it should be worth trying. A richer life, better work, the experience of success and its rewards: those ends are surely worth one experiment in procedure.

All the equipment needed is imagination and the willingness to disturb old habit-patterns for a while, to act after a novel fashion long enough to finish one piece of work. How long that period is will vary, of course, with the work to be accomplished, and whether it is all dependent on oneself or of the unwieldier type which the executive and administrator know, where the factor of other human temperaments must be taken into account.

In any case, some results from the experiment will be seen at once. Often these first results are so astonishing that to enumerate them here might alienate readers of a sober habit of mind. To hear of them before coming to them normally would be like hearing of miracles, and some of the effectiveness of the program might be lost by the intrusion of the very doubts we are out to banish.

Once more: however remarkable the results, the process is straightforward and uncomplicated. It is worth trying, for it has worked in hundreds of lives. It can work in any life that is not more truly dedicated to failure than to success.

Chapter 2 - The Will to Fail

FROM the disciples of Schopenhauer and Freud, of Nietzche and Adler, we have all become conversant with such phrases as the Will to Live and the Will to Power.

These phrases, representing---sometimes to the verge of overstatement---drives of the organism towards fulfillment and growth, correspond to truths of experience with which each of us is familiar. We have seen children struggle to make themselves and their personalities felt; as young people we have contended for a chance to try our own emerging forces; after long illness we have felt the tide of returning strength in our veins. We know that any average man caught in unfortunate circumstances will put up with poverty, distress, humiliation with conditions which an onlooker will sometimes consider as much worse than death; and that only the presence of a will to continue living can account for the tenacity with which a man in such circumstances clings to the mere right to breathe and exist.

Furthermore, we first experience and then later turn to realize the process of growth in ourselves. The individual, emerges from childhood into adolescence, from adolescence into maturity; and at each of these crisis we find that the activities and interests of the old period are being replaced by those of the new, that Nature is preparing the organism for its new role in the world, is actually reconciling us to the new demands on us by showing us pleasures and rewards in the oncoming state which will replace those we must abandon.

But the idea of another will, a counter-balancing will, the Will to Fail, the Will to Death, is not so readily accepted. For a while it was one of the tenets of psychoanalysis, for instance, that no individual could actually imaginatively encompass the idea that he might cease to be. Even the death-dreams and suicide threats of deeply morbid patients were held to be grounded solely in ideas of revenge: the explanation was that the patient thought of himself as living on, invisible, but able to see the remorse and regret caused by his death in those by whom he thought himself ill-treated.

Freud, indeed, analyzing shell-shocked patients after the War, issued a monograph in which he stated that he had occasionally found dreams that indicated sincere death-wishes. This monograph is full of some of the best of Freud's speculations and suggestions; but as for the appearance in popular psychologies of the idea that there could logically be a deathward current running through our lives, it is as though the thesis had never been suggested.

Yet death is as much a fact of experience as birth and growth; and if Nature prepares us for each new phase of life by closing off old desires and opening new vistas, it does not seem too difficult to think that we are, always, being slowly, gently reconciled to our eventual relinquishment of all we hold dear as living creatures. And withdrawal from struggle, abandonment of effort, releasing of desire and ambition would be normal movements in an organism which was being gently wooed away from its preoccupation with life.

It is for this reason that we are entitled to look upon the Will to Fail as a reality.

Now, If inertia, timorousness, substitute activity, effortless effort, quiescence, and resignation were found only at the end of life, or when we were drained by sickness or fatigue, if they never handicapped us when we should be in the full flood of our vital powers, there would be no reason at all for attacking this Will to Fail as if it were---as indeed it is---the arch-enemy of all that is good and effective in us. But when it appears in youth or full maturity it is as symptomatic of something wrong---deeply, internally wrong---with one's life as untimely drowsiness is symptomatic of ordinary bodily ill health.

And if it were easily seen for the black-hearted villain it is, when it arrives out of its due time, it would be easy to fight. But almost always we are well within its power before we do more than suspect rarely and vaguely that all is not as it should be with us. We are so accustomed to speak of failure, frustration, timidity, as negative things, that it is like being invited to fight windmills when we are urged to fight the symptoms of failure.

In youth we seldom recognize the symptom; in ourselves. We explain our reluctance to getting started as the natural timidity of the tyro; but the reluctance stays, the years go, and we wake in dismay to find that what was once a charming youthful diffidence in us is now something quite different, sickly and repellent. Or we find a convenient domestic situation to bear the brunt of excusing us for never having got to work in earnest. We could not leave this or that relative lonely and defenseless. Then the family grows, scatters, and we are left alone, the substitute activity at which we had been so busy is taken remorselessly away from us, and we are sick and terrified at the idea of turning back to take up the long abandoned plans.

Or we have the best of all reasons for not doing as well as we might. Most of us are under the necessity of choosing between work and starvation, and the employment we were able to find when it was imperative that we should begin earning is not work for which we are ideally suited. When marriage and the raising of a family have been undertaken, the necessity is all the more urgent. We might be willing to wait through a few thin years if no one but ourselves would suffer, but to ask others to do so takes more selfishness, and more courage, than most of us can muster.

Especially in America, where marriages for love are the rule, most young people start out on their married life with little more than their health, youth, and intelligence as capital. We are accustomed to think of the European idea of asking a dot, a dower, from the bride's family as somehow ignoble and mercenary. Yet insisting on that little reserve fund of money with which to meet the demands of establishing a new household has much to recommend it, and the fact that we have no such custom in this country may be one reason why America, the much-vaunted Land of Opportunity, can show so many men and women of middle age wasting themselves in drudgery, filling positions which bring them no joy, and looking forward to a future which at its happiest promises years of monotony, and at its worst the nightmare of poverty-ridden unemployment.

This necessity to fall upon the first work we can find is alone enough to explain why so few of us ever manage to bring our plans to fruition. Often, at first, we have a firm intention of not losing sight of our real goal, in spite of the fact that we must make a living at uncongenial work. We plan to keep an eye on our ambitions, and to work at them by hook or crook--- evenings, weekends, on vacations. But the nine-to-five work is tiring and exacting; it takes super-human strength of character to go on working alone when the rest of the world, is at play, and when we have never had any evidence that we should be successful if we continued, anyway. And so without realizing it we are swept into the current of the Will to Fail. We are still moving, and we do not see that our motion is down stream.

Most of us disguise our failure in public; we disguise it most successfully from ourselves. It is not hard to ignore the fact that we are doing much less, than we are able to do, very little of what we had planned even modestly to accomplish before a certain age, and never, probably, all that we had hoped. One reason it is so easy to deceive ourselves is that somewhere along the way we seem silently to enter into a sort of gentleman's agreement with our friends and acquaintances. "Don't mention my failure to me," we tacitly plead, "and I will never let the hint that you are not doing quite all I should expect of you cross my lips."

This tactful silence is seldom broken in youth or in the early middle years. Until then, the convention is that at any moment we may get into our stride. A little later and the silence is relaxed. There comes a time when it is safe to smile ruefully and admit that the hopes we went out to meet the world with were too high and much too rosy, particularly those hopes we had held for our own performance. In the fifties---and sometimes earlier---it is usually safe enough to do a little disarming and semi-humorous grumbling; after all, few of our contemporaries are in a position to say "Why can't you start now?" And yet some of the greatest work in the world, many of the world's irreplaceable masterpieces, were done by men and women well past what we too superficially consider their prime.

So we slip through the world without making our contribution, without discovering all that there was in us to do, without using the most minute fraction of our abilities, either native or acquired. If we manage to be fairly comfortable, to get some respect and admiration, a taste of "a little brief authority" and some love, we think we have made a good bargain, we acquiesce in the Will to Fail. We even pride ourselves on our shrewdness, not suspecting how badly we have been cheated, that we have settled for the compensations of death, not the rewards of life.

If the elaborate game that we all play with ourselves and each other never came to an end---never ran down for a moment so that we suddenly saw that it was only a game after all---the Will to Fail might urge us all gently downhill till we came to rest at its foot, and no one would dream of protesting. But the game has such a way of breaking off sometimes, right at its most amusing spot; and we suddenly wonder why we are running about like this, how we happen to be playing away at hide-and-seek as if our lives depended on it, what became of the real life we meant to lead while we have been off doing nothing, or busy at the work that provides us with no more than our bread and butter.

Sometimes the moment passes and is forgotten until long after, if ever remembered at all. But some of us never forget it. If we go on with the game, it turns into a nightmare, and how to wake out of it and get back into reality becomes our whole preoccupation. Then sometimes the nightmare seems to deepen; we try one turn after another which looks as if it led to freedom, only to find ourselves back in the middle of Alice's Looking Glass Garden beginning the hunt all over again.

Yet we can escape; and again, rather like Alice, by seeming at first to go backward: by admitting that there may be a real Will to Fail, and next, that we may be its victims.

Chapter 3 - Victims of The Will to Fail

IF the Will to Fall announced its presence with symptoms as uniform and unmistakable as those which indicate measles or a bad cold, it would probably have been eradicated, or a technique for combating it would have been worked out, long ago.

But unfortunately its symptoms are varied and legion. If you were to drag a dining, dancing, theater-going, middle-aged metropolitan playboy away from his merry-go-round and introduce him to an unshaven, ill-clad cracker-box philosopher dreaming in the sun, saying, "I want you two to know each other; you have so much in common," you would be thought mad, yet you would be right. The dreaming idler, the introvert, and the dancing extrovert---at the antipodes from the point of view of worldly circumstance---are motivated by the same impulse; unconsciously they are both trying to fail.

Their lives have a common denominator. "Do not act as if you had a thousand years to live," Marcus Aurelius warned himself in his maxims. All those in the grip of the Will to Fail act as if they had a thousand years before them. Whether they dream or dance, they spend their precious hours as though the store of them were inexhaustible.

But since there are as many ways of failing as there are divisions and subdivisions of the psychological types, we often do not recognize the presence of the Will to Fail in others or in ourselves. Here are a few of the innumerable ways of "acting as though you had a thousand years to live":

There are, for instance, those who sleep from two to six hours a day more than they need to sleep to keep in perfect physical health. In any individual case, unless the sleeping hours far exceed the normal quota, it is very hard to be sure one has not to do with merely an unusually long sleeper. But when the note of compulsion enters, one can be sure of having found a true victim of failure. Those who are bad-tempered or only half alive if an early bedtime must be postponed, those who anxiously count each morning the exact number of hours spent in sleep the night before, mourning inconsolably any interruption, every hour of insomnia, every untimely doorbell, are looking to sleep for more than its normal restorative function. When an adult extends even this, making a nap or two a day a matter of routine, the diagnosis becomes simple.

Next, still among the inconspicuous failures, the "introverts," are the waking sleepers: persons who allow some activity to pass before them almost without participation, or indulge in time-killing pursuits in which they take only the most minor and unconstructive parts: the solitaire-players, the pathological bookworms, the endless crossword puzzlers, the jigsaw puzzle contingent. The line between recreation and obsession is not hard to see once we know it is there.

Easiest of all to recognize as lovers of failure are the heavy drinkers. A volume could be written on them, but too many volumes have. Where drinking is so constant as to bring on a waking sleep, or, deeper, a kind of death in life, the presence of the Will to Fail is obvious to any observer. But there are thousands who show the symptoms in so faint a form that they pass almost unnoticed: all those who drink knowing that it means a bad morning the next day, a vague and woolly approach to every problem until the effects have passed off; those to whom any drinking means physical discomfort, whether acute or trifling. Anyone who has learned to expect these consequences and yet continues to lay himself open to them stands convicted of the desire to handicap himself, at least to that extent. It makes very little difference what the drink in question may be. If coffee disturbs you, if you cannot digest milk, and you nevertheless continue to drink it, you may escape the disapproval which is meted out to the highball drinker, but you are in the same class. And, plainly, unwise eating comes under the same head.

Turning to the active type, it may be said that the extroverts who pursue failure as their primary career find so many ways of doing it that the attempt to tabulate them all would be hopeless. But, as examples, there are the relentless movie- and theater-goers, the nightly dancers, all those who count the day lost which has not a tea or dinner or cocktail party in it. . . No, of course there is nothing against relaxation and recreation when they are really called for, after a period of contributory activity. But those who enter an objection to this classification too early and too angrily, crying that one must have recreation, give themselves dead away as setting an abnormal value on release.

Then there are the half-and-half failures, difficult to place, such as the embroiderers and knitters, although it is only fair to say here that sometimes a light task calling for only manual dexterity may go on while the mind is usefully engaged in solving a real problem. Complete honesty with oneself is all that is necessary to discover whether the rhythmical activity is being used in one way or the other. If a dull stupor sets in, or if, on the other hand, the work is just elaborate enough, calls for just enough conscious attention so that no automatic rhythm can be established, then it is rare indeed that this kind of motion can be put in the category of true creative activity, or that of being accessory to creative action.

As to aimless conversationalists, we can more easily see others fall in that group than that we are included ourselves. Sometimes we are startled into realizing that we have repeated the same anecdote to the same friend and for a few days go warily. That is a minor slip. No reminiscent ring, no forced smile on our auditor's lips will stop us when we are habitually marking time with words - when we have the same unevolving round of topics, the same opinions to repeat mechanically, the same half-aimless observations to make on the same recurring situations, the same automatic indignation at the same old abuses, the same illustrations to prove the same points, and a few lukewarm arguments to bolster up what may once have been opinions but are now seldom more than prejudices.

Sometimes we ride a verbal mannerism so hard that a hearer objects irritably.

(Suggestions for overcoming such mannerisms will be given later; here we are only considering the way in which they unconsciously betray in us the presence of a Will to Fail.) It is probably a great piece of luck to rouse a friend to this extent. If you learn with shocking suddenness that you are forever saying "I mean," "Of course," "I imagine," "Do you see?" "You know," "As a matter of fact," you are likely to listen to your own voice for a period and discover that not only do these tag words occur over and over in your conversation, but that there is nothing particularly fresh or valuable about the ideas they have served to embellish. Here, as in the other categories, it is very easy to see that there is something wrong when one meets gross examples of the difficulty; an hysterical talker is obviously mentally ill. But that there are subtler forms of the same trouble, often hidden for years because we do our repeating to constantly changing audiences, seldom dawns on us.

There are still more obscure and unnoticeable ways of falling victim to the Will to Fail, ways to which introverts and extroverts are almost equally susceptible. Consider the innumerable persons, for instance, who deliberately undertake work which calls for only a small part of their abilities and training, and who then drive themselves relentlessly, exhausting themselves over useless details. There are the takers of eternal post-graduate courses, turning up on the campus year after year like so many Flying Dutchmen.

There are the "devoted" daughters and sons and mothers and wives (fathers are seldom found here, for some reason, although there may be an occasional husband) who pour out their lives into the lives of other adults, but whose offering, since they have never truly developed what was most valuable in themselves, adds no richness and only unimportant comfort to the objects of their "self-sacrifice." There are those who undertake a task known by them to be beyond their powers, or engage in a specious "research" problem: there is a man in New York, for example, who has been gathering biographical details about an obscure Italian statesman since his sophomore year in college. This pseudo-biographer is now in his late forties, and not one word of that definitive Life has been written.

Perhaps the greatest class of all those whose goal is failure is that of the Universal Charmers. When you find yourself in the presence of more charm than the situation calls for, you are safe in saying to yourself, "Ah, a failure!" This is no diatribe against genuine warm-heartedness, against friendliness, or true sweetness of character. We are talking now about the Harold Skimpoles of the world, about the cajoling, winsome adult, either man or woman, who insists on being accepted by his or her contemporaries as just a great, big, delightful child--- irresponsible, perhaps, not very thoughtful, but so exceedingly lovable, even to strangers! There are the whimsical teases and the humorous complainers, and if they are good to look at, quick-witted or amusing, they are more likely than not to be successful in arousing a momentary indulgence, a tolerant tenderness.

It is only in retrospect that one realizes there was no valid reason for the moment's emotion. A healthy adult does not need the tenderness or indulgence of every casual acquaintance. Except for a guilty conscience, no one would ever dream of making a play for this kind of response. These victims are under the hard necessity of working at charm as convicts work at stone-crushing; they must go on being more and more charming to offset their waning attractions, or face the truth--- admit that they have not adequately discharged their responsibilities. As long as their inadequacy is never seen except mirrored in the indulgent eyes of another they can go on without admitting the fact that they are failing. So on they go, cheating their way through life---unless by good fortune they can come to see who really suffers most from the exercise of their charm.

So there are all these ways, and innumerable others, of filling one's time with seemingly purposeless activity, or a falsely purposeful routine, and they are all the result of submitting to the Will to Fail.

For, remember, these activities are only apparently purposeless. There is in every case a deep intention, which may be stated in many ways.

We may say that the most obvious intention is to beguile the world into believing that we are living up to our fullest capacity. This is particularly true of those cases where the outward life is full of a thousand little matters, or one big job of drudgery conscientiously done. No one, surely, could ask us to do more than we are doing? Are we not plainly so busy that we have not one minute or a grain of strength to do anything more? Is it not our duty to do the dull, insignificant, unsatisfying task thoroughly? Those are questions which only the individual can answer honestly for himself, usually in the hours of insomnia or convalescence, when the mind which is usually so engrossed about trivial affairs finds time to stop and consider.

In the long run it makes little difference how cleverly others are deceived; if we are not doing what we are best equipped to do, or doing well what we have undertaken as our personal contribution to the world's work, at least by way of an earnestly followed avocation, there will be a core of unhappiness in our lives which will be more and more difficult to ignore as the years pass.

The fritterers and players and the drudging workers are bent mainly on deceiving themselves, on filling every nook and cranny of their waking hours so that there is no spot where a suspicion of futility can leak through. And at night, of course, they are either still hard at play or too exhausted to consider realities. Yet such victims present a dreadful spectacle when once they are plainly seen---seen as insane misers, stuffing a senseless accumulation of trash, odds and ends of sensations, experiences, fads and enthusiasms, synthetic emotions, into the priceless coffer of their one irreplaceable lifetime.

Whatever the ostensible purpose may be, it is plain that one motive is at work in all these cases: the intention, often unconscious, to fill life so full of secondary activities or substitute activities that there will be no time in which to perform the best work, of which one is capable. The intention, in short, is to fail.

Chapter 4 - The Rewards of Failure

ABSURD as it may seem at first consideration that anyone would solemnly enter into even an unconscious conspiracy to fail, it is a matter of observation that there is hardly one person in a hundred who does not, in some fashion, deliberately cripple and thwart themselves. To understand why this should be so it is necessary to examine for a chapter what may be called, without paradox, the rewards of failure.

The recent widespread interest in all branches of psychology has accustomed us to accepting an idea which, when first offered, seemed laughable: that we are all at some level, engaged most of the time in reverie. We dream either consciously or unconsciously, awake or asleep, of a situation in which we feel we should be happier than we are in real life. Occasionally some childish idea of happiness or success crops up to confuse or hamper us in the business of adult living. Sometimes the dream is of a life of luxurious idleness, the childish Unconscious determined on refusing to leave the safe shelter of the nursery, where all wants were remedied as soon as felt, where warmth and food and love were given freely and unearned. As Emerson wrote, long before we had any technical vocabulary to express that backward turning reverie, long before we knew of "fixations" or of "narcissism" "We do not believe there is any force in today to rival or recreate that beautiful Yesterday. We linger in the ruins of the old tent where once we had bread and shelter." To some extent this is true of all of us, but less true of the happy and successful adult than of others.

At other times, ludicrously enough, the life-wasting reverie is about success: the mild man is a Napoleon of war or finance, the mouse-like woman a siren. If reality never broke in upon such reverie, the dreamer might be happier, self-absorbed in their silent tale-spinning, than if they were to find themselves in a position to realize some part of it. Such reverie is in itself compensation for a life of dull routine or uneventful monotony. But, the world being what it is, the dreamer must live, for part of their time at least, in the cold atmosphere of fact. This is no Land of Cockaigne that we inhabit: roast pigs do not run about crying "Eat me!" Fruit does not fall from the trees into our mouths. However blissful the daydream we entertain, we must wake from it sometimes and struggle with the hard conditions of real living.

The inveterate dreamer will struggle only just as much as he need, and no more. He will do anything halfheartedly to get his bread and butter. Then, when his daily task is over, he will be back at his dreams again, whether he realizes it or not. He succeeds at only one thing: in clearing away a little space, gaining each day a few hours of free time, for just one purpose---to go on wasting his life. But his dream is happy. It is, for him, a true compensation for his failure in every other relation, and so he continues in it. Yet, since after all happiness is the true goal, he is deluded by not realizing that the smallest success in reality brings with it more happiness than years of reverie.

Nevertheless it is important to remember that the rewards of failure are real in their own sphere, for otherwise we will not brace ourselves to fight them adequately; and there are other rewards of failure besides dreams.

Consider, for instance, that if you try for anything just enough to give yourself some justification for saying that you have tried, you can fold your hands for the rest of your days. You can say humbly that you were tried and found wanting in those qualities which make for real success. This is rather a rare remark, but one of those which can be heard now and then from older failures, usually in a humorously deprecating tone. It will sound very honest and touching; and there is no earthly way in which it can be proved against the complainant that his statement is not fully true.

He has saved himself a lifetime of effort by some means, nevertheless. If you join this group you can watch the struggles of others with an eye half-amused, half-envious, enjoying the results of their successes, but perhaps even more---human nature being what it is---the spectacle of those who fail, and who take up their onlookers' positions beside you.

Then, "Mankind is very superficial and dastardly," as Franklin said. "They begin upon a thing, but meeting with a difficulty, they fly from it discouraged"; and why not, asks the Unconscious, when you can try, stop, and feel for the rest of your life that if you had tried just once more you would have made the grade? You can thereupon become a dilettante or amateur, frightfully hard to please by those who go on working, severest of all critics either professional or unprofessional, possessor of some inner knowledge, and able to hint at standards of excellence untouched by those who are still out trying to run the dusty race; standards so marvelous, so unattainable, that failure to reach them is more honorable, you may imply, than another man's easy success. With not one thing completed, the acclaim you might have received, the enormous financial coup you might have brought off, the masterpiece you might have accomplished, can assume in your reverie, and in the eyes of those who will accept your version of things, almost more importance than the real success would.

Or you can become an abettor and sustainer of more persistent workers and artists, and perhaps that is the friendliest failure, the most successful failure, of all.

But notice that in all these cases you will at the very least have avoided the struggle, the pain, the humiliations that attend outward activity. You will never have to see the object you slaved to bring into being despised or misunderstood. You will never have to feel the rancor of those whom you necessarily surpassed in competition; you will never have to stand the cut of adverse criticism. You will never have to become aware of the malice of those who envy any success, however trivial. You will never have to back your opinions by argument when you are tired and would rather rest for new effort. Or, far deeper and more vital pain, you will never see the discrepancy between the finished work you can do and the work as you had hoped to do it. There is always that discrepancy to keep the honest worker really humble.

These matters of discomfort and pain evaded are important to notice, for when we come to examine the reasons why we so often choose to fail rather than to succeed, they will prove very illuminating. So it is worth understanding that if you fail, you are rewarded by not running the risk of getting hot and tired and discouraged, or sharp-tempered when your co-workers or your materials, whatever they are, seem more refractory than usual. If someone else does excellently in the line you had dreamed of for yourself, you can always believe that, if you had really tried again, you could have surpassed them.

And then, if you can remain inconspicuous, you will not have the experience of outstripping someone you love. This is, perhaps, most commonly the woman's Reward of Failure, although the children of distinguished parents or the disciples of outmoded masters in any line also know it. Still, it is only right to say that many who dread the experience of causing pain to another are never called upon to meet it; they failed to take into account the generosity of love. So it is often an excuse for not working that is at the root of this inaction, too, not a real matter of compromising with ambition in order to keep a vital relationship unspoiled.

By failing one escapes much gossip and incomprehension, the semi-scandalous talk which most often springs up about those who succeed. To dread this immoderately is neurotic, but this dread does often act as a deterrent to many a success. All vital persons are the target of the curiosity of those who are not vital; but the few whose opinions concern you will know the truth, and the others are of no importance. Yet many withdraw from active life, not to take up an intenser inner life, but merely to avoid the vulgar curiosity of the crowd.

And then, if you have failed not too awkwardly, you are usually more delightful as a companion than a better worker. Those who reach real success are likely to be constant workers. Even in their hours of recreation they frequently are preoccupied with some element of the thing they are engaged in doing. The successful man has less free time, and observes more punctiliously his self-set hours for withdrawing from companionship, than the failure. He can seldom be counted on for impromptu gaieties, since he is not unconsciously intent on finding any escape at all from the unsatisfactory conditions of his life. And, since he has none of the deep interior guilt which haunts the one who knows he is failing, he is under no compulsion to be winning. He reserves his humor and charm, his emotion and indulgence, for those whose lives are closely bound up with his by his own choice. So, except among his real intimates, he may have the name of being gruff and unapproachable, or too coolly civil. As long as you cannot bear the notion that there is a creature under 21 heaven who can regard you with an indifferent, an amused or hostile eye, you will probably see to it that you continue to fail with the utmost charm.

Perhaps it will be helpful to look for a while at three lives in which the Will to Fail was at work. In every case the onlooker would see a life of considerable activity, such obvious activity that he would at first glance be likely to agree with the victims that they were in the grip of a perverse fate. On closer examination, each failure will be seen to be by no means determined by any factor outside the individual character.

Each of these persons had within himself or herself the abilities necessary to make a full, happy, productive life; each spent what energy they had on defeating their ostensible intention: one saw her mistake and rectified it, one died without facing the truth about his wasted talents. The third is still struggling with his problem, as far from success as ever, though his name is well known.

Case 1 is that of a woman, left a widow while she was still very young. She came of a scholarly family, and had been a brilliant student at college. With the little money left to care for herself and her small daughter, she returned to the campus to take degrees as Master of Arts and Doctor of Philosophy in preparation for a career as an educator.

Actually (as she found to her astonishment when her difficulties became so great as to force her to seek advice) she delighted in being a student again, in continuing to live in the condition of a child in an adult world, and therefore strung out her period of preparation as long as she dared. After her .D. was earned, she made what looked to herself and her friends like a good honest effort to find a suitable niche for herself.

Only she invariably engaged in wrangling acrimoniously with those who would have to be her superiors, and always about some rather remarkable and original economic ideas of her own. These ideas had nothing whatever to do with the subject she was to teach; their acceptance or rejection by the entire world would not have made one grain of difference in the class-room work which she was called on to perform; but by making an issue of having her absurd and quixotic ideas taken seriously by her co-workers, she brought about---each time she found a position---a situation in which she was distinctly disliked by the very persons on whose goodwill she was dependent.

She went from one post to another, never holding one longer than the year for which she had contracted. She was a good teacher, a well-informed student, and she had much to give, but she carefully saw to it that she would never be in a position to work very hard for very long. Her hopes of a professorship faded. She went from good colleges steadily downgrade to obscure little schools, and as she slipped steadily down she worked out a philosophy which reconciled her to her steady decline. She held that we all live much too luxuriously, and put too high a value on becoming clothes, good food, and comfort. At last she reached the place where she felt justified in taking an apartment in a tenement district of a large city. Her defiant self-justification broke down, however, when it came to inviting friends to visit her. She grew more and more solitary, more and more eccentric, her running fire of bravado continuing all the while.

Fortunately for her, her one child was a girl, and a girl who grew up to be extremely bright and attractive. She was quite unimpressed by her mother's pseudo-philosophy; she knew that she was being handicapped at every turn by the oddness of their living and dressing, and as she emerged into adolescence she began to fight for a more reasonable life, a suitable background. Matters came to such a pass that either the mother had to take cognizance of the girl's objections or lose her daughter. All the efforts to correct her false position which she made by herself were unavailing. She still brought about the old wrangles whenever possible, she still held the unsatisfactory position to which she had dropped only on tolerance and because she had come to accept a very small salary, in spite of her training and ability.

When at last she sought help from a psychologist she discovered to her dumbfounded astonishment that she had actually thrown all her energy into failing. Unconsciously she had resented having to go out into the world to work. She wanted to remain either a child or become again a cherished and petted wife. Her wrangles had been, as the analysts say, "over-determined": they were intended partly to make it certain that she would be discharged so that work would become impossible, partly to engage the attention of men. Since she could not acknowledge to herself that she was cold-bloodedly "husband-hunting," she had fallen on the technique---quite as effective in challenging attention as being charming---of starting quarrels. She had a long, hard pull to right the situation she had brought upon herself, but she was eventually successful.

Case 2 is such a one as can be found in almost every town and village in the country, a failure of the sort that is not only treated tenderly, but often looked upon as being in some vague way much nobler and finer than any success. It was that of a man with a good mind, noted for his integrity and yet not without a vein of good Yankee ingenuity. He lived and died in the small town of his birth; a rather ugly little manufacturing town. Not because he loved it loyally and wanted nothing better; his reading was always of travel and adventure, and he continually spoke wistfully of countries and places he had never seen. Not that he had no opportunity---opportunity came and tried to hound him into activity. He was the manager of a branch store of a large business, and so satisfactory at it that he was offered a similar position in a larger city, at a correspondingly better salary. He accepted with joy; then within two days he wrote a letter saying that he had reconsidered, that he did not believe that he could fill the better position. His timidity grew on him. A few years later he was combating every improved method that his firm tried to introduce, afraid to try the new ways. A little later he was such an obstructionist that his firm retired him on a minute pension, and he became the town's lovable homespun philosopher.

A senator spoke movingly at his funeral; his fellow townsmen were inconsolable.... Perhaps it is deplorably callous to point out that his wife had preceded him to the grave by ten years, worn out with overwork; that one son had no education beyond what he could get at the village school, although he had as good a mind as his father; that the other son had to work his way through college, thus dividing his energy and strength (for it is only one more fallacy of the American creed that to work one's way through college is the ideal way of getting an education); that his daughter had taken refuge in a loveless marriage from a home that had never had enough of the ordinary comforts or attractions.

Let us be perfectly plain about one point: to hold that honest success is in some way ignoble is one of two things---pretense or cant. There is a tyrannical effort to impose this fallacy on us, arising perhaps from a confusion of the mere word "success" with the idea of a great fortune arrived at by fair means or foul. But that there is anything ignoble in accomplishing well what one sets out to do, and in receiving in return rewards in the shape, sometimes of the approval of one's peers, sometimes the quiet knowledge that the world is richer for one's contribution, or sometimes in money paid out gladly for an object or services fully worth the price to the purchaser---such an idea is nonsense, and the very opposite of what it is usually claimed to be, "philosophical." William Ernest Hocking, in his excellent book, Human Nature and Its Remaking, has this to say on that very point: "If command of the fruits of the earth is the normal and destined position for man, why should one who has achieved such a position, and in so doing has shown large powers of one kind or another, not receive the recognition that he, in so far, has succeeded? It is a man's work to make a fortune, and under normal circumstances a measure of ability." Many who know Case 3 by his name would protest loudly at his appearance here incognito as an illustration of the Will to Fail at work. He is a writer, and the son of a writer. From the first he has been under such a fortunate star that he knows almost nothing of the long struggle for recognition which is so often the prelude to a literary career. Nevertheless, at one and the same time he lives in terror of failure and in the grip of an instinct which seems to drive him in that direction. He will not work until he is desperate for money; then he will write like mad, tiring himself till he is poisoned with fatigue, and acts afterwards like a convalescent.

Trying to overcome this bad working-habit under the advice of a psychiatrist, he attempted to work, more than once, when there was no urgent necessity for money. In those circumstances he invariably turned out stories which were unacceptable until rewritten. The world knows nothing, of course, of those wasted efforts, that time spent on the disheartening revisions which he is constantly called on to do. Each time this occurs his career seems drearier and less glamorous to him, his belief that he can eventually write a book he will not be ashamed to sign with his name grows dimmer. Here again analysis brought some illumination as to the unconscious reason for this action, and again the tendency to do haphazard and unsatisfactory work was over determined: there was on the one hand a dread of surpassing his illustrious father at the same profession, on the other the sly unconscious notion that if the stories he seemed to slave over were rejected he would not have to work at all, and would be free to dream through his life in his own way. For the Unconscious always refuses to understand that reality must be taken into account, refuses to admit that "work or die" is the rule the average mortal must live by.

Yet this tormented man recurrently has an experience which might, if he could comprehend it, show him the way out of his dilemma: when he is at last desperate for money, when he cannot go any longer on credit or the indulgence of his friends, or his reputation, when, in short, he has the courage of desperation, he writes material which is immediately accepted. Instead of drawing the workable conclusion from this fact, he has made it an item of superstition: only work done, as he says, "at the thirteenth hour," is ever lucky for him! So he continues on his treadmill.

Now, in each of these cases, failure, or comparative failure, brought its reward with it: escape from adult effort and time to waste in day-dreaming. Only in those cases where frustration was more painful than success was there any attempt to reshape the life-pattern.

Do you feel that obviously those who waste life in this way are at least mildly insane? We all make similar difficulties for ourselves, avoid work, miss opportunities. Have you ever looked back and thought, "If I had done this or that five years ago I'd be better off now?" But the opportunity was there; why didn't you see it? Are you sure that you are not closing your eyes at this moment to one which you will see later in retrospect? Is the Will to Fail not operating in your own life every day? Yet the rewards of success are so immeasurably more worth having. Once more, the smallest task well done, the smallest object, out there in the world where it would not have been if you had not acted, brings in a moment more satisfaction than the failure knows in a lifetime. The knowledge that one is being tried by a real scale and not by the shifting standards of reverie is like having land underfoot after weeks of drifting at sea. Only those who are at work on the best they can do are free from the danger of panic-stricken awakening to reality--- awakening sometimes so late that the very habits and attitudes of normality are forgotten.

And, beside the innumerable purely subjective advantages, there are the rich objective rewards. A dream-picture brings no buyer, a dream-plan no dividends, a fantasied book is followed by no royalty statements. Crass as this may sound in a world which spends a great deal of its breath in persuading futilitarians that they have chosen the better part, it is the literal truth and stands for a truth still greater. Fantasy may call the grapes of reality sour, but those who have tasted them know at last a dependable delight.

Chapter 5 - Righting the Direction

What this highest idea is will vary from individual to individual, and will expand with growth. No outsider can dictate another's private definition of success. It may, it often does, include some recognition from one's fellows, and greater financial rewards; on the other hand, it may not. Many a researcher in the sciences would consider himself fully successful (and would be right), if he added one minute fact to the mass of accumulating details on which science must proceed, if he took one item out of the realm of hypothesis and speculation and placed it in its proper relation to the mass of known truths. His name might never be known by those outside his science; it might be quite obscure even within his own field. He would nevertheless have attained the goal for which he was working if he accomplished that which he himself set out to do.

The actress who reaches the top of her art is as successful as the mother who raises a large and healthy family---but not more so. A priest or minister immersed in the care of his parish lives as successful a life as the genius whose name is known by most of his contemporaries. Another's ideal of success may have so little in common with our own that we are quite blind as to what he can see in the career he has chosen, but unless we are totally unimaginative we know, when we see him living responsibly, effectively, usefully, happily, making the most of his advantages and gifts, that we are dealing with a successful man.

To offer too circumscribed a definition of success would defeat the purpose of this book. Much of our distrust of the word, as it is, comes from not realizing the infinitely extensive range of possible "successes." Each of us, usually by late adolescence, has a mass of knowledge about himself, which--- if we took the counsel "Know thyself" seriously---could be examined and considered until the individual's ideal of the good life would emerge from it plainly. It ought to be part of education to see that each child should understand the necessity of finding this clue to his future, and be shown that it is sometimes thrown into confusion by hero-worship, or by the erroneous notion that what is an item in the success of one must be present in the success of each of us. Still, in spite of confusion, false starts, the taking over of the ambitions of a parent or teacher for ourselves instead of finding our own, most of us do arrive in the early twenties knowing what we are best fitted to do, or could do best if we had the training and opportunity.

It is worth noting carefully that unless you have allowed yourself to overestimate your character grossly, your own success-idea is within the region of those things which can be brought about. Usually, far from overrating our abilities, we do not understand how great they are. The reason for this under-estimation of ourselves will be considered later, but it is well to realize that few except the truly insane believe themselves suited for careers far beyond their full powers.

The next point to understand is that in these pages we are not talking about success of any secondary or metaphorical sort. Your idea of what is success for you is not here to be replaced by another high-sounding, "idealistic" compromise. You are not being exhorted, once more, to lower your hopes and then find that you can easily reach the simpler standard. Such programs are only temporizing with failure. On the contrary, the more vividly you can present to yourself the original picture of the goal you once hoped to be able to reach, the better your chances are of attaining it.

Now, having examined the currents in our nature which lead us to acquiesce in failure, understanding that, if we allow it to happen, we can be carried unprotestingly down in the deathward direction, let us see what is operating immediately to keep us from the healthy efforts we must make to succeed.

To do so we must turn to a subject which is in some disrepute today: hypnotism. For many reasons, some excellent but others suspiciously weak, hypnotism is a subject which is seldom studied nowadays. If you have never had occasion to read a sound book on the subject, it may seem to you that some of the feats claimed for hypnotized persons cannot possibly have been done. There is some likelihood, however, that you have read at least one book on auto-suggestion, the method of healing which was so popular about a decade ago, and auto-suggestion is one of the by-products of the nineteenth-century study of hypnotism.

But few readers today know of the work, for instance, of Esdaile in India in the middle 1800's: of the surgical operations he performed painlessly on hundreds of patients, of his comments on the rapid recovery of those who had felt no pain during the operation---an early contribution to the theory of the deleterious effects of "surgical shock." The work of Braid and Bernheim is almost unknown, and Mesmer, who combined a fantastic theory with a mass of arrestingly effective experiments, is now looked on mainly as a quack.

There is no doubt that hypnotism is in its present disrepute partly because its early practitioners could not refrain from premature and fantastic theorizing, and because it became connected in the minds of the public with such subjects as "spirit-rappings" and "slate-writing" mediums, many of whom were later exposed as tricksters.

Possible experimenters were alienated from the subject because it was offered to the world with such unnecessary accompaniments as the hypotheses about "odic fluid" and "animal magnetism"---explanations which explained nothing. In addition to these prejudicial theories, experiments in anesthesia by the use of chloroform and ether were proceeding in the same years. Insensitiveness to pain reached by hypnosis was uncertain and presented many difficulties: not everyone was hypnotizable, and, even more important, not every physician was able to hypnotize. Inevitably, the more certain form of attaining anesthetization through the use of chloroform and ether was the practice which became accepted.

The study of hypnotism, which many acute observers of the middle and late nineteenth century believed to be the first step towards the freeing of mankind from physical suffering, as well as the overcoming of many temperamental difficulties and the cure of many vices, fell into a decline. With the emergence of the psychoanalytic theory, the defeat of hypnotism---at least for our day---was cemented.

Now, although the formula that we are about to consider has in it no trace of auto hypnotism, it is still possible to learn from the despised procedure what it is that defeats us in our efforts to be effective. Consider for a moment the successes of a good hypnotist with a good subject: they sound utterly beyond nature, and for that very reason we have not learned from them all we might garner. One man, ordinarily suffering from vertigo at even a slight eminence, when hypnotized can walk a very narrow plank at a great height. Another, looking light and delicate, can lift a dead weight. A stammerer can be commanded to give a fervid oration, and will do so without showing a trace of the speech-defect which hampers him in his normal state.

Perhaps one of the most remarkable cases is one cited by F. W. H. Myers in his chapter on hypnotism in Human Personality: a young actress, an understudy, called upon suddenly to replace the star of her company, was sick with apprehension and stage-fright. Under light hypnosis she performed with competence and brilliance, and won great applause; but it was long before she was able to act her parts without the aid of the hypnotist, who stationed himself in her dressing room. (Later in this same case the phenomenon of "posthypnotic suggestion" began to be observed, and the foundations of the Nancy school of auto-suggestion, of which Coué is the most famous contemporary associate, were laid.)

In the same chapter in which he quotes the remarkable case of the actress, Myers made a theorizing comment which is of immense value to everyone who hopes to free himself of his bondage to failure. He points out that the ordinary shyness and tentativeness with which we all approach novel action is entirely removed from the hypnotized subject, who consequently acts instead with precision and self-confidence.

Now the removal of shyness, or mauvaise honte (he wrote), which hypnotic suggestion can effect, is in fact a purgation of memory---inhibiting the recollection of previous failures, and setting free whatever group of aptitudes is for the moment required.

There is the clue. No sentence was ever more packed with rich implications for those who are in earnest about reorienting their lives towards success.

It has become a commonplace to say that we learn by "trial and error." We learn by discovering that one course of action does not bring about the end we had in view; we try again, and perhaps many times, until we find the procedure which accomplishes our intention. We then adopt the last term in this series of acts.

That is the mental picture we make of the "trial-and-error" method of learning.

Roughly it is right, but it omits to emphasize one element of the process which, although we may not dwell upon it intentionally, is never forgotten by the Unconscious: the element of pain. We believe, or speak and write as though we believed, that the one success remains as the total residue of the series of attempts, and that it cancels from our minds all the failures which went before it. We do not take into account the tremendous importance to our future conduct of those discarded trials which ended in failure. We succeeded at last, it is true; but meanwhile we experienced failure, sometimes ridicule, sometimes real pain, sometimes grave humiliation. We by no means retain in our memories only the item of the final success, nor does the success operate to make the failures and pain unimportant to our Unconscious.

The Unconscious dreads pain, humiliation, fatigue; it bends its efforts even more ceaselessly to the end of avoiding pain than it does to the procuring of positive pleasures. So we are faced with a fact which at once accounts for much of the inactivity, the inertia, to which we succumb at moments when positive action would be to our advantage: that rather than face the mere possibility of pain we will not act at all.

Rather than revive the memory of our early failures, let alone run the risk of hurting ourselves anew, we will unconsciously decide to remain inactive, or we will choose to do something easier than we should attempt, or we will start on a program and carry it near the spot where we were hurt before, and there find any excuse to beat a hasty retreat, leaving the work undone, the reward ungathered. The childish Unconscious wins: at least we were not bruised again in an already tender spot.

It is utterly illogical, of course; in order to avoid a trivial discomfort we roll up a great account of failure to wound us in the future, we miss opportunity after opportunity which may never come again, we expose ourselves to far greater pain than that we manage to avoid. But at least the memory of that early humiliation can sleep, or only turn restlessly, half-awakened.

Now, if that is true---and only a little self-analysis will prove that it is true---how convenient it would be if each of us could carry a hypnotist about, to cast his spell whenever we had to get to work! How marvelous if each of us could have his own private Svengali! Impossible, of course; and, more than that, undesirable. Fortunately, it is not at all necessary to be put under the sway of another's will in order to do our own work.

The solution is far simpler. All that is necessary to break the spell of inertia and frustration is this:

Act as if it were impossible to fail.

That is the talisman, the formula, the command of right-about-face which turns us from failure towards success.

Clear out, by an easy imaginative feat, all the distrusts and timidities, all the fears of looking ridiculous which you may hardly suspect of being treacherous troublemakers in your life. You will find that if you can imaginatively capture the state of mind which would be yours if you knew you were going towards a prearranged and inevitable success, the first result will be a tremendous surge of vitality, of freshness.

Then---well, the only way to put it is that it will seem as though your mind gave a great sigh of relief, of gratitude for the liberation, and stretched itself to its fullest extent. This is the moment where one may be forgiven for feeling that there is something truly magical about the whole affair. There will appear an extension of capacity which seems more than normal.

Then the long-dammed-up flow sets in: directly, irresistibly, turned at last in the right direction, the current gathers strength from minute to minute. At first you may still harbor some fear that the spell which worked so instantaneously may break in the same way. It will not, simply because it is no spell; it is a reminder to yourself of the way in which work can always be successfully undertaken. If you remember that, far from your seeing the successful action stop, you will find that each hour of unhampered activity opens out into a promise of others in the future. There may actually be some embarrassment from seeing too many expanding possibilities until you have learned to organize your new life.

Those fears, anxieties and apprehensions, you see, were far more than mere negative things. By acting as if they were important, you endowed them with importance, you turned them into realities. They became parasitic growths, existing at the expense of everything that is healthy in you. While we allow them to sap us, we are allowing the nourishment which should go towards expanding growth to be used for feeding monsters, cherishing the freaks and by-blows of the mind instead of its extraordinary and creative elements. So that it is not that one is suddenly given wonderful new powers; by ceasing to let fear hold its frustrating sway we come into the use of already existing aptitudes which we formerly had no energy to explore. We discover that we already possess capacities we had not suspected, and the effect, of course, is as though we had just received them. And the rapidity with which these capacities make themselves known when once the aspects are favorable for them is truly somewhat startling. It is even more enjoyable.

Next, there is the further experience of seeming to become, in contrast with one's old self, practically tireless. Actual records of working periods introduced by using this formula would strain the credulity of those who have never yet had the experience. And these periods are not followed by any depressed reaction. There is always so much ahead, and it is so clearly seen, that there is no chance for depression to set in when the mind is turned back from its onward drive to consider all the tribulations of the past, all the possible mischances which might conceivably happen, it cannot, of course, at the same time explore the road into the future. But once absolve it of the thankless and unnecessary task, and it rewards you by seeming to fly where before it had stumbled and groped.

It takes some self-education to learn how to go from one item of successful work to the next, not to lose time and spend strength---much more happily, but just as surely---in gloating over either the ease with which the task as done or in contemplating too fondly the truly remarkable work one has just been so fortunate as to produce. But a few days' Harvest Home is quite excusable; and since, still resilient and unexhausted, one looks forward to further activity with enjoyment, there is no permanent danger that the first success under the new regime will be the last.

If you are tempted to look askance at this procedure, to feel that you arc being invited to deceive yourself into a feeling of success, you are quite wrong. We are all pragmatists and empiricists in our daily life; what "works" for us is our practical truth, and becomes the basis of our further activity. "Our thoughts become true in proportion as they successfully exert their go-between function," as William James says. And even more fully and convincingly, the late Hans Vaihinger worked out these conceptions in his book, The Philosophy of "As If." Not everyone will go with him to the furthest boundaries of his theory, but it is certainly plain that in most matters of life each of us must act as if this or that fact were a self evident truth. For one thing, if we insisted on proving the reality or efficacy or even probability of most of the conceptions on which we base our practical procedures, we should have no time left in which to act. So, in general, we accept the premises for action which are presented to us on good authority, and use them as proved unless or until our experience causes us to doubt the wisdom of so doing. Then we may reexamine them and perhaps reach different conclusions from our mentors, but for the most part we all act as if our norms of conduct, our standards of values, were eternally and everywhere valid, so long as they prove practicable for us.

In everyday life, then, if you are ineffectual in your daily encounters and unproductive in your work, you are to that extent acting as if you willed to fail. Turn that attitude inside out, consciously decide that your "As If" shall be healthy and vital, shall be aimed towards accomplishment, and you have made success a truth for yourself.

"The law of nature is: Do the thing and you shall have the power; but they who do not do the thing have not the power."

Chapter 6 - The System in Operation

IF you are the possessor of a very vivid imagination, you will probably be already well on the way towards practice with no more than the clue in that sentence: Act as if it were impossible to fail. If you are not, or if you have been badly hurt by failure, there may be some difficulty in beginning to act effectively, but there need not be very much.

To get at it more slowly, the idea is just this: instead of starting wherever you are---or, to be accurate, instead of trying to start, or swearing that you will start, or deceiving yourself into thinking that you are going to start tomorrow or the day after--- beset by all the usual doubts of your own performance and memories of past pain, take time first to "make up" your state of mind, the mental condition in which you are going to work.

If you have an important appointment you do not rush out to it unkempt, unwashed, in any old clothes. You take some trouble to make yourself look as well as you can. Man or woman, you brush and clean your clothes, you look for your good points and emphasize them, you hide or improve your blemishes. Then, when you go to your appointment, you try to act as much as possible as if that heightened condition were your normal state.

Now, you are mentally going to an appointment, an appointment with your successful self. How can you arrange your frame of mind to make that appointment fruitful? You first give yourself a model. Everyone has had a taste of success in some line, perhaps in a very minor matter. Think back to it, however childish it was, even if it was a success of your schooldays. It needn't be, even remotely, success in the adult work you hope to do. What you want to recapture is the state of mind in which you once succeeded. Be careful, now; you do not want to overshoot the mark. Don't jump ahead into the elation which followed the success itself. Just recapture the steady, confident feeling that was yours when you knew the fact that was demanded of you, when you realized that you could do the thing that was necessary, that what you were about to do was well within your powers.

Try to bring back as clearly as you can every surrounding circumstance of that moment. Now transfer in imagination that success-sequence to the work in hand. If you were absolutely certain that everything about the present work would go as smoothly as everything went when you succeeded in the past, if you knew that what you are beginning would certainly go well, from the moment you begin till the moment of the work's ultimate reception, how would you feel? How would you act? What is the state of mind you would be in as you launch out into it? Fix your attention on that, for that is to be your working frame of mind. Until you can reach it, refuse to begin; but insist to yourself on reaching it as soon as possible.

When you have found the mood hold it steadily for a while, as if waiting for a word of command. All at once you will feel a release of energy. You have received from yourself your working orders, and you can begin. You will see that you no longer have to push yourself to do the work; all your energy is free to push the work alone.

It was that extra, unnecessary labor of pushing your own inertia aside which made it seem, before, that you were too hampered to get started, were groping through a fog to get at your object, or were stopping continually to brush away half realized doubts, anxieties, memories of failure that buzzed about you like a cloud of gnats. Clear all that away before you begin to work by the simple expedient of refusing to contemplate the mere possibility of failure.

Next, work till you feel the unmistakable onset of true fatigue. True fatigue. The early flagging of attention will be only the old state of mind trying to creep in once more when your attention is elsewhere. If that happens, stop a second and say to yourself, "No. That is the way I will not think!" clear out the impulse entirely, and go on working. When your muscles and your mind honestly protest that they have done all they should do for the time, stop and find some relaxation. If you are held by office hours, go away quietly alone for awhile when the old state of mind seems in danger of returning, or when you find that you are going to have to spend some time in altering the attitude of a fellow worker before you can move smoothly in the new way. Stay alone until you have reestablished your confident attitude, then return to the group.

When the time for relaxation comes you will find that you get the full joy of playing at last.

There are some persons who have been so badly bruised that, although any unwarrantable indulgence towards oneself should be guarded against, it may be necessary to begin this system by practicing it only for a short time each day, and on some secondary desire. Most educators agree that the best way to teach a child to act confidently and competently, and to facilitate the process of learning, is to ask him first to perform some small task which is well within his untrained powers. As Dorothy Canfield Fisher says in her excellent little book for parents and teachers, Self-reliance, "Success or failure in adult life depends largely on the energy, courage and self-reliance with which one attacks the problem of making his dreams come true.

Self-confidence in any enterprise comes as a rule from remembrance of past success." And, again, Professor Hocking in Human Nature and Its Remaking: "Education consists in supplying the halted mind with a method of work and some examples of success. There are few more beautiful miracles than that which can be wrought by leading a despairing child into a trifling success; and there are few difficulties whose principle cannot be embodied in such simple form that success is at once easy and revealing. And by increasing the difficulty by serial stages, the small will, under the cumulative excitement of repeated and mounting success, may find itself far beyond the obstacle that originally checked it."

So in our own cases, when self-confidence has been lost, should we find some little desire which for some reason has never been gratified. There are scores of these opportunities in every life. All that is necessary, in these experiments toward success, is either that some desire should be taken from the realm of dreaming into that of realization, or that a procedure which was not the perfect one for the effect to be produced should be corrected.

You remember the immortal Bunker Bean, and how his life changed when he was persuaded by the fraudulent medium that he was the reincarnation of a Pharaoh? His rise in the world was rapid; one success followed another and brought a third in its train. When at last he knew he had been cheated, that he was no incarnation of Rameses, nor was the mummy case that had been sold him made of wood that ever saw ancient Egypt, he had so learned the technique of success that he could not slip back into obscurity. If you observe any family likeness to H. T. Webster's Mr.

Milquetoast in yourself, it might be worth your while to get Bunker Bean and reread it; the time will not be wasted, since it is only a little less funny than it is fundamentally true.

Here are some examples of developing secondary talents so that confidence in important matters follows:

There is a notably successful physician in New York who recently learned to model in clay, and went on to learn the coloring and glazing of pottery. He did it with the direct intention of giving himself the experience of success in an avocation, since his profession, which is psychiatry, calls on him to deal constantly with refractory material. The confidence which he gains in one line is carried over into his difficult daily work; and in addition he has an engrossing hobby which freshens his mind and has become one more source of approval, since his modeling has come to be always amusing and frequently really distinguished. He must have had a great deal of talent, you may think. Well, what he did have was the knowledge that he had always been attracted by the idea of modeling; he had never touched clay until he was in his thirties. He simply took a desire which almost everyone has felt at some time or other and turned it into a source of pleasure and added self-confidence.

Again, in the Art Institute of Chicago there is a room called by the name of a business man who learned to paint after he was fifty. His work, entered in a competition in which his name could not possibly be known, took a first prize. There is now a club of middle-aged business and professional men in Chicago who are studying art and producing good work.

A thirty-year-old clerk in a business office who had had no early advantages had wanted all her life to play the piano. One day on her walk home, moved by an impulse which she fortunately did not resist, she turned into a house which advertised music lessons by a little sign in the window. Her success, of course, is only comparative. She has not the time needed to make a really excellent musician, nor did she begin early enough to train the special muscles that a professional pianist uses.

But she succeeded in reference to her own goal. Her whole life has been altered by that moment of courage. Besides the pleasure she has had from understanding music as only the performer can ever understand it, she has, and knows she has, acted in an adult fashion which resulted in giving her more confidence in every relation of her life. From being the over-worked and oppressed drudge of her home, she came to live in her own small apartment, she visits her family on terms of amicable indifference, and has made a group of friends whose tastes coincide with hers.

These three cases should give a hint, at least, of the proper procedure. Take a definite step to turn a dream into a reality. Say, for instance, that you want to travel and have never been able to do so. When this dream is to be removed from the region of dreams to the region of reality there are several things which must be done. If you are not doing them, you are giving yourself good evidence that you are letting your infantile unconscious dictate the terms of your living rather than your rational mind.

If you want to see Italy, for instance, you will certainly enjoy Italy better if you can speak a few words of the language, read a current newspaper in Italian, or know of Italy's past. Do you? Yet there are many excellent small grammars, phrasebook and histories; and how better can you get started than quietly to buy one of these? What else will you need? Time and money. Well, reverse the usual phrase and say to yourself, what is certainly true, that money is time: that if you have a fund of money on which to travel you have also a fund of time. Start in to get it. Put asides small coin each day, but don't stop there. Think what work you can do in your spare time that will bring you a little more money for your journey. If it is nothing more than to sit with children while their parents are at parties, and if you think of the payment as absolutely dedicated to your intention to travel, you will be acting towards a successful life.

A young and hard-worked assistant editor, wanting to travel, found his way to the offices of an Italian newspaper printed in New York, there received help in translating an advertisement he had written into Italian, in which he offered to exchange lessons in English or in journalism for lessons in Italian. Two years later he went to Italy as tutor companion to a young boy, and today he is secretary in a minor capacity in the diplomatic service: the goal he always had in view for himself, but had for years considered unattainable because he had to live up to the very edge of his financial margin.

Be careful that you do not turn these first steps into merely a more elaborate way of playing the old game of daydreaming with yourself. Do something every day towards your intention, however remote your goal may have to be. If you like to model, stop at a ten-cent store and buy plasticine tomorrow; if to travel, write for folders; at the very least, if you have no money to spend at all, you can go to, or get into correspondence with, the nearest public library, and learn to use the expert services of librarians.

At first say as little as possible to others of what you intend to do. Get an effect before beginning to talk. If you talk too soon you may almost come to feel that there is a conspiracy against your doing anything out of your usual routine; you will be at least partly right. Those who are still slaves to dreams, to the Will to Fail, are made uncomfortable by the sight of anyone who is breaking free. They feel that there is in the unwonted action some criticism directed at themselves, and become uneasy. At any moment, the Unconscious knows its supremacy may be disturbed, its opportunities for reverie taken away from it. So it begins to fight. One of the most universal forms this combat taken is that of quotation; maxims which sound wise, but which are usually only self consolatory, spring to the lips of those who reject reality.

"The skies change," they will say to you, sententiously; "the heart remains the same," but they will not be quoting in the sense of the original. Or "The grass is always greener on the other side of the fence" you will hear, from those who cannot be bothered to look beyond their own front yards. And so the subtle process of undermining your enthusiasm, and bolstering themselves in their own opinion, will go on. If proverbs fail, they will fall back on teasing.

Now you, if you are at last tearing yourself free, are entering into a conspiracy with Reality, an agreement to see how much may be got out of life if you act with a little more directness and courage than you have used before. Don't put yourself into a position to be discouraged at the start, or bullied out of, or teased about, your new program. Within a short time the results of your action will speak for themselves, providing you with all the justification you need.

Always your first question to yourself should be, "What would I be doing now if it were really impossible for me to fail at---

whatever it is: traveling, modeling, writing, farming?" It may be any of these things, or any one of a hundred more: to dance, or dress-make, study calculus or Greek, become better looking, or hear more music.

Whatever it is, by thinking, you can discover easily what the first step would be if you were engaged with reality, and not with a dream of a different life. Now you are engaged with reality; take that first step. Then ask yourself the next, and so on until you see the ambition itself taking form in your life, beginning to grow with what looks like independent growth, beginning to carry you along instead of having to be searched after. For that is what happens: at a certain stage you will find that you are being borne along swiftly and easily on the momentum started by your own initial actions. "Life is infinitely flexible," an old analyst used to say to his patients; and while that may be a little excessive, it is true that life is far more malleable, more flexible, than it seems to be so long as we are unwilling to act.

Or there is another way of starting to act successfully. We seldom realize how great an amount of the friction we all undergo in our lives comes from our expecting to be rebuffed or ignored. Think back to some encounter you had today in your office, in a store, with a servant or tradesman in your home. Try to remember just the form your request took. Making all due allowances for courtesy, or for the respectfulness due to superiors and elders, was there not in addition a tentativeness about your request? Didn't you ask for cooperation in such a way as to leave room for refusal, or grudging action, or for being ignored? Now, think of the ideal way in which that question could have been asked, or that order given. It can be cast just as courteously as before, but in such a way that the person of whom you asked help cannot refuse you without being deliberately surly and hostile.

That is the tone of success. When you find it you benefit not only yourself, but the person with whom you must cooperate for effectiveness. Do not waste another's time and energy or your own patience by suggesting even indirectly that there is more than one course of action, if there is only one which will get the result you require. The work to be done takes half the time if the attention is undivided and so is free to go on to the next demand quickly.

Have you ever been in an office where, let us say, a worker who considers herself rather too well-bred for the position she fills is one of your coworkers? "Oh, Mr.

Robinson," she will say, elaborately, "if you have just a moment to spare, will you go over those reports on your desk some time soon? I hate to trouble such a busy man, but Mr. Smith wants them." Now, deplorable or not, it is just plain ornery human nature to wish you hadn't just a moment to spare, to cast around you almost automatically for something else you might be doing which would make you far too busy to get to that request right away. Yet probably going over those reports is the next thing on your program, anyway; if you succumb to the temptation to hold up the work and teach the ex-countess a lesson, you hold up the whole work of the office and get into trouble with your superior officers. Now, wasn't your time and energy wasted by the unfortunate way that simple request was made? Yet the chances are that you yourself say, "Miss Thomas, will you get me the Drummond correspondence, if you aren't too busy?" when it is Miss Thomas' function to get the correspondence at your request whether she is otherwise busy or not; when she will have to say "Certainly," and pretend that she is free to refuse if she likes. It would be just as simple to say, "Miss Thomas, I need the Drummond correspondence"--- which would release her to go straight to the task, feeling that she was not receiving a consideration more than half-patronizing, and not even needing to make a perfunctory reply. If the tone of the simpler sentence is courteous and considerate you have not only left her feelings unwounded, you have treated her as your willing coworker and given her cause not to think of herself as a touchy subordinate who must be mollified.

These seem such minor matters, but it is the sum of small things successfully done that lifts a life out of bondage to the humdrum. Women are particularly subject to using the wrong tone to subordinates or office associates, and many of the charges that women are discriminated against in business come from the fact that quite unconsciously they import a mistaken polish into their everyday affairs. Women who complain nightly of incompetence or insolence from maids or children, office girls who have serial stories to tell of impertinence or "office politics," are, in almost every case, the ones really at fault. By approaching their human contacts with the wrong attitude, by using the wrong tone and the wrong words, they open the way for differences of opinion which never need arise.

By going over your day in imagination before you begin it, thinking of all the contacts you are likely to have and how they can best be handled, listening to your own voice and correcting it till you get the tone which is at once courteous and unanswerable, you can begin acting successfully at any moment. By doing so you will find that you get through your business day with less fatigue; with what you have left you can begin to realize some minor wish of which you have long dreamed in secret.

From there it is only a step to finding the courage to begin to do the major things which you have wanted and hoped to do.

Chapter 7 - Warnings and Qualifications

BEFORE going further, it may be well to issue a few statements as to what this system does not include.

The advice is not to hypnotize yourself into success. This is important to understand, for many people, and with some reason, dread and fear anything that is based on hypnotism, even in the form of self-suggestion. The work of the Nancy school, with which Coué made us all familiar, is full of excellent hints for self-management, and Charles Baudouin's book, Suggestion and Auto-suggestion, can be read to great advantage by many who do not follow him with full agreement; and there are several small handbooks on Coué's system which are worth studying. But it is not for nothing that the fad which was once so widespread has faded away. In spite of all warnings, too many of those who attempted self cure ended by reinforcing the troubles they set out to banish.

No, although a sentence from a chapter on hypnotism was helpful in discovering our formula, the connection of this procedure with hypnotism ends there. You are advised to use, first, a minimum of will---just enough to decide to try a new process. Then, as in the Nancy school, the imagination takes over until your mind is clear, cool, and "pleasant" in tone; not confused, diverted, troubled or foggy.

The difference lies just here: in intensive auto-suggestion there is a serious danger that the mind will get as out of touch with reality in the other direction as it was in its day dreaming or depression; that it will become, as the French say, exaltée, a word for which we have no exact and satisfactory equivalent. But "extravagantly elated" is about what exaltée implies, a state of mental intoxication as dangerous as it is temporarily delightful. You cannot live on those peaks; and if you could, you would, again, find yourself unable to act effectively in the world of reality. Without such action you are as far from success, as deep in self delusion, as ever.

Confident, steady, freely flowing action is what we need. Then safe delight begins.

The mind, cleared of its doubts, begins to expand and enjoy its own activity; the rewards of satisfactory action begin to show themselves. An elation which has nothing to do with delusion or hypnotism naturally follows, and has no later reaction to nullify it.

Second, the advice is not to make "affirmations" such as "I cannot fail," "I am successful in all I do," and so on. This procedure, which is helpful with many, has too much in common with auto-hypnotism for those who do not thoroughly understand the principle on which they are working as they follow it. There is much to admire in the philosophy behind those religions which use "affirmations"; that there is an ultimate Unity behind the duality or diversity of the world seems an inescapable conclusion. Nevertheless, we are "conditioned" (as both Behaviorists and philosophers say) by the flesh, by personality, by the concrete world; so we must at least act as if the constitution of the world were dual, almost evenly distributed between good and evil. Most of us are brought up short by prosaic commonsense when we try to use the "affirmative" method, and for one who can successfully make use of it there are a hundred who feel ludicrous when doing so. There are others who succeed for a while and then find themselves worse off than before. There is no disapproval whatever for the method when used by those for whom it is, we might say, temperamentally suitable. But for skeptics of even a mild order, it is likely to be more irritating than helpful.

Thirdly, the advice is not to dash out and impress others by posing, pretending or downright lying about one's successfulness. The only one to impress, at least at first, is yourself, and that only to the extent of making for yourself a congenial working atmosphere.

 The recommendation, once more, is simply this: Act as if it were impossible to fail.

Then, above all, you are not advised to engage in still one more fantasy about success, a somewhat more detailed and circumstantial fantasy than you have pushed yourself to before, but still bearing signs of its kinship to your former day dreaming. In this case the use of the imagination is quite different, and worth a little detailed scrutiny later.

Long before Freud made his contribution to modern thought, Pico della Mirandola, in a treatise called De Imaginatione --- Concerning the Imagination --- was discriminating between two kinds of reverie: the one retrograde, backward-turning, keeping the man from his man's work, prolonging irresponsibility and mental childhood; the other, the true imagination, was found in the successful man.

An aphorism of Joubert, which denies the fine name of Imagination to the former type of reverie, is perhaps the neatest definition that can be found, worth pages of ordinary "distinguishing": "Fancy," he says, "an animal faculty, is very different from imagination, which is intellectual. The former is passive, but the latter is active and creative."

It is the latter creative imagination which is to be called on, and if that fact is kept fully in mind there will be no danger of slipping once more into the bad old habit of dreaming the world into a different shape while life slips away. Remember again that "Success depends on a plus condition of mind and body, on power of work, on courage." It is that idea which must be held firmly in mind: that the test of whether or not one is dreaming or imagining correctly is whether or not action follows the mental work. Any mental activity which turns backward for longer than it takes to correct a mistake and to replace an unsatisfactory habit with a good one, is minus, and cannot be continued if you hope to lead a fuller life.

You set for yourself in advance the hours in which you will work. Within those hours, and as part of that work, you first clear and free your mind. When this has brought you to a pleasant, confident, quiet state you are ready to get at the work proper. The first part of the time is spent clearing the decks for action. You clear the decks; you act.

Now, this is an age of alibis. We all know a little too much about the Glands Regulating Personality, and the Havoc raised by Resistances, and so on. Never since the world began were there such good opportunities to be lazy with distinction. It is perfectly true that many cases of subnormal energy can be helped by the proper glandular dosage, but how many of those who have spoken to you of being probably hypothyroid[1] ever went through the simple process of having a basal metabolism test to see if that were really the trouble? Of course they can claim that the situation is so grave that they cannot even get up energy to start being cured; there's no answer to that one.

1

But if you are really seriously handicapped by lethargy, you can take your first success-ward step by consulting a good diagnostician, if necessary. If necessary, mind; for there is a fact which makes a good deal of the talk about glandular insufficiency look like the alibi it too often is, and which will be confirmed for you by specialists in glandular therapy if you ask them: that if those who complain of lethargy increase their habitual activity little by little the glands respond by increased secretion. In short, very often this condition can be cured by starting at the other end! You may rest assured that you will have no consequent breakdown in following this advice unless you deliberately (and with intent to cripple yourself) leap from a practically comatose state to one of manic activity.

As for Resistances! They are almost an item of dogma in the current secular religion.

Persons who would never dream of going to the time, expense, or trouble of a full analysis will tell you complacently that they have "a resistance" to this or that, and feel that they have done all and more than can be asked of them by admitting their handicap. Remarkable cures of resistances, however, have been observed in those who took solemnly the advice to replace that word with our ancestors' outmoded synonym for the same thing: "bone-laziness." It is not quite so much fun, nor so flattering, to be foolishly lazy as it is to be the victim of a technical term, but many are crippled for knowing an impressive word who would have had no such trouble if they had lived in a simpler and less self-indulgent society. Those who are genuinely, deeply, and unhappily in the grip of a neurosis should turn at once to one of the well known therapies. Unless one is willing to do so, it should be made a matter of social disapproval to refer technically to such difficulties.

If the alibis of the age were in any way generally helpful, if they were not excuses for remaining inactive, and if inactivity were really a happier state than effectiveness, there would be little harm in indulging in the contemporary patter, even without the specialized medical or psychological knowledge necessary for using the terminology correctly. But before you decide that you are the victim of uncooperative glands, or a villainous Resistance, try a few of the suggestions for self-discipline in a later chapter.

You may find them so much fun, your expanding powers so much more rewarding than---well, your bone-laziness---that you will not need the services of an expert, after all.

Chapter 8 - On Saving Breath

EARLIER in these pages the advice not to talk has been given. In fact it may seem that I believe one of the prerequisites for success is to sink oneself into a surly silence.

Nothing can be farther from the truth. To talk enough, to talk persuasively, to establish and maintain friendly relations with those around us, is of supreme importance to effective living. Nevertheless, it is easy to talk too much, at the wrong times, or with the wrong objective. Innumerable proverbs exist to show that folk wisdom has always recognized a danger in excessive wordiness. "Speech is silver, silence is golden"; "Much talk, little work"; "A barking dog never bites," we say; we call the tongue "the unruly member," say that a gossip's tongue is "hung in the middle," speak of a demagogue as "a windbag," praise "a man of few words," and are sometimes uncomfortably impressed by the strength of laconic speech.

Without making too much of a point of the matter, a few of the reasons for counseling silence may be worth examining. Every great religious discipline insists on the wisdom of learning the control of speech. Several Christian sects observe silences; some are vowed to perpetual silence. One of the greatest and most famous philosophical religious systems, that of the Indians, devotes an entire phase of its training not only to controlling speech, but to controlling breath: the Pranayama of the Hindus. In Latin the word for breath and the word for soul are masculine and feminine forms of the same root, in Greek they are identical.

There is more in this than meets the eye of the reader who is always on the run.

Breathing is one of the few involuntary actions of the body over which we can exercise voluntary control. That is to say, it is on the borderline between the regions of the conscious and the unconscious. The man or woman who can speak or be silent as he chooses is the individual who has self control.

When the Unconscious has us fully at its mercy we talk not as we should voluntarily choose to talk if we could see all the consequences of our speech, but from a need to relieve some half-perceived pressure. So we grumble humorously about our difficulties, and make ourselves self-conscious by doing so. Or we excuse ourselves defiantly. Or we complain of a trifling injustice, and are sometimes startled to see how much more pity we invoke than the occasion warrants. Once we have found a wellspring of pity and indulgence in another, we are seldom mature enough not to take advantage of it, thus reinforcing our infantilism and defeating our growth.

One of the worst wiles of the Will to Fail is that it forces its victim to ask for unnecessary advice. Here again the universal deep motive for asking advice(unnecessarily, it should be emphasized once more) is that by so doing we can go on feeling protected and cherished even though we are no longer children. But that again means that we are being provided with advance excuses for failure. If we act on the advice of another and are unsuccessful, obviously the failure is not ours but our counselor's; isn't that plain? So we can continue to daydream of successful action, to believe that if only we had followed our first impulse we could not have failed.

Since such motives can be present, it is wise to scrutinize every impulse to ask for advice. If the origin of the desire is above suspicion, then there is only one further question to ask before seeking help with a clear conscience: "If I worked this out for myself, would I consume only my own time?" If the answer to that is "Yes," then it is generally better to work out the problem independently, unless the amount of time so expended would be grossly disproportionate to the importance of the result.

If you are a creative worker, remember that time spent in finding an independent technique is seldom wasted. We are accustomed to think of the success of a man like Joseph Conrad, a Pole, in writing the English language, or of the work of an electrical genius like Steinmetz, as savoring of the miraculous. To have had to work out their problems alone--- what a tremendous obstacle to overcome! On the contrary; the necessity for independent action was one of the conditions of their success, and to see and admit this is in no way to detract from the worth of their accomplishment.

Most of us support each other and are in turn supported to such an extent that we can make almost no individual contribution; the final result of our labors is a sort of olla podrida, a medley of tastes, talents and techniques, with little to differentiate it from similar results. Look, for a moment, at any of the run-of-the-mill novels of the day; at the layout, wording and illustration of the advertisements in any given magazine; at the comic strips in a number of papers. Would it seem too far-fetched to say that although one man, one woman, or one firm is actually behind each of these bids for our attention, they all seem to have been issued from a sort of central bureau? Yet however uncomplainingly we absorb these issuances from the Ministry for Novel Writing, the Central Bureau for the Production of Comic Strips, the Committee in Charge of National Advertising, we save our real rewards for those who bring us freshness or genius.

So the working out, however laborious, of an original technique is worth the time expended, the loneliness entailed. With that well in mind, let us consider those times when advice should be taken.

You have a genuine problem. The first step, then, should be to write it out, or to formulate it verbally with exactness, so that you can see just what it is that is troubling you. If you simply let the problem wash around in your mind, it will seem greater, and much vaguer, than it will appear on close examination. Then find your-expert, whether friend or stranger, but make every effort to find one whose views seem to be congenial to you, since that usually implies similar or congenial mental processes. To do so earlier will mean that you are wasting both your time and his by making him the audience of part of your self-examination. If you are successful in getting an interview, make that as short and concise as possible while still covering all your points. Then follow the advice you are given until you see definite results. If you are tempted to say "Oh, that won't work for me," then you should suspect your own motives. Such a rejection implies that you already had a course of action in mind, and were more than half-hoping that you would be advised to follow it. Watching an example of the wrong attitude towards advice and instruction here may be more illuminating than any positive example.

Have you ever seen the teacher of an art class at work? Frequently he will find in the drawing of one pupil a flaw which is so typical of most students' work at the same stage that he will call the other pupils of the class around the easel. Using the imperfect canvas as his text, he will branch into criticism, advice, exhortation, and will occasionally go on to rub out the mistake and draw the line or put in the color as it should have been done. If you will observe the group at this moment you will discover that, tragically enough, everyone seems to be benefiting by the lecture except the very pupil to whom it should be most valuable. In almost every case the one whose work is providing the example will be quivering, nervous, sometimes tearful, often angry---in short, giving every sign that he is feeling so personally humiliated and insulted that he is reacting at an infantile level. If you ask for help, or put yourself into the relation of a pupil to a teacher, learn to advance by your mistakes instead of suffering through them. Keep your attitude impersonal while you are being shown the road back to the right procedure.

If you are in school, or taking class or private instruction, it is wise to take every opportunity to ask well considered questions, then to act on the information, and finally---and very important---to report to your instructor as to your success or failure through following his advice. This is of advantage not only to you, but to him and his subsequent pupils, since he cannot know what practices are effective and what are only useful to himself and a few like him unless his pupils report in this fashion. If you must consistently report no progress, then one of two things must be true: that you are not fully understanding him, or that you are not working under the right master.

After your period of apprenticeship is over, try not to weaken yourself or bring about self-doubt to such an extent that you must have help on minor points of procedure.

Every physician and psychiatrist knows that there is a great class of "sufferers" who return again and again, asking so many and such trivial questions that it seems unlikely they could ever have grown to maturity if they were as helpless in all relations as they show themselves to their physicians. No one except a charlatan truly welcomes the appearance of such patients as these. The person who is looking for an excuse to blame his failure on another or who will not, if he can help it, grow up and settle his own difficulties, will go on asking advice until he draws his last breath, and even the astutest consultant may be forgiven if he sometimes mistakes an infrequent questioner for one of the weaker type.

A good touchstone to show whether you may be only following a nervous habit of dependence is to ask yourself in every case: "Would I ask this if I had to pay a specialist's fee for the answer?" All busy persons whose work brings them into the limelight have frequent requests for personal interviews. Usually they answer as well as they are able, taking much trouble rather than run the risk of rebuffing any talented or sensitive beginner; but they are ruthlessly exploited. When, as sometimes happens, an eminent man comes to the place where he answers no questions of this sort, it is not that he is swollen with conceit, not that he would not gladly help anyone in genuine perplexity, but that he has no certain way of winnowing the sincere inquirers from the neurotics, and, since he still has his own valuable work to do, he reluctantly decides for silence. To console himself he knows that many who are ready to do their own work only frustrate themselves by acting with too much humility, and that if their questions go unanswered they will find their own satisfactory solutions.

So talking, complaining, asking advice, inviting suggestions--- all are better abandoned during the period of reeducation. Ultimately and ideally, of course, you want to be able to work under any and all circumstances. You cannot ever be certain that your favorite confidante or your most stimulating friend will always be in a position to lend a sympathetic ear at the moment that you feel you need it. If you establish the habit of going to someone at a certain point in your work, and lead yourself to feel, even unconsciously, that this is necessary to a satisfactory performance, you are laying the foundation of future failure.

Moreover, whatever your field may be, if you spend every possible moment at creative activity, you will come to the place where you have a body of your own work, a total of experience, to consider; you will get the "feeling of your material." Then you will see how many of your problems arose because you had previously been in the position of an amateur or novice, because you had so little experience in your own line that for a while every problem seemed unique.

Chapter 9 - The Task Of The Imagination

ALREADY imagination's contribution to a productive life has been considered somewhat, and its help has been called on in the matter of making that favorable mental climate which is necessary if we are to produce our best work. But imagination has innumerable other uses, it can be helpful in ways so diverse that the same faculty hardly seems to be in operation in all of them.

In everyday life, we tend to think of the imagination as something which may, perhaps, be spoken of as "useful" to artists of all sorts, but as being almost the opposite of useful in the lives of practical men and women. To use one's imagination, generally, is thought of as taking a holiday, as allowing the wits to go woolgathering, the mind to relax and sun itself. After indulging it---for we commonly think of the exercise of the imagination as being in some way an indulgence---we may return refreshed to the commonplace, or we may find we have lost time, missed contacts, got out of step with our companions and helpers: in short, suffered for allowing one part of the mind free play.

As a consequence we look warily at the imagination, often seeking to check it, or, in some extreme cases, even eradicate it. That it can be of immense benefit in the most prosaic affairs is an idea at which many readers will balk. But that is because they do think of the imagination as a faculty which always wanders unchecked, which must be permitted to make its own rules and occasions, which is incapable of being directed, and, to a great extent, controlled---put at the service of the reason and the will. Thus controlled and directed, it becomes the mature creative imagination, the spiritual faculty of which Joubert speaks.

But consider a few of the many things which it can usefully do for us: it can help us to stand away from ourselves somewhat, holding the emotions and prejudices which often keep us from seeing clearly well in hand. By so doing we may find that we are thwarting our own best interests constantly, and can replace the disadvantageous activities---still in the imagination---by others which will bring about happier results.

It can be turned on the character of an opponent or an uncooperative "helper" while we study him as an author might study a character whom he hopes to place in a book.

We can get clues to his motives, and thereafter watch to see whether we have been right about them, thus saving ourselves from such mistakes as being too brusque with a sensitive person, or too laxly indulgent with another who will exploit us if we give him or her the opportunity.

Nor does this begin to exhaust the ways in which imagination, instead of betraying us into reverie and resignation to unsatisfactory conditions---instead, even, of being employed merely as a means of recreation---can contribute to the making of a good life. Working as far as possible under orders from the will, and hand-in-hand with reason, it can explore new fields for our efforts, can bring back to us some of our original freshness towards our work which we have lost by fatigue and routine; it can even perform such a severely practical function for us as to discover new markets for our wares, or new ways in which to use old talents.

These ideas are worth a little closer examination here, and later the insertion of some exercises in using the imagination.

We need not belong to that group which, as we say, "can only learn by experience." Having discovered that much of our dread of engaging in new activity comes from unconquered fear of the pain which we formerly met when we began to go forward, we can decide that some of our "trial-and-error" attempts at managing life shall go on in the mind, in the imagination, where it is, to all intents, painless. We can learn to look ahead imaginatively, and so save ourselves from blunders, ineffectuality, loss of energy and time.

First of all, we can use imagination to see ourselves and our work in some perspective.

Everyone knows how a child identifies himself utterly with all he owns and does, with all those who care for him. He is outraged if asked to share his possessions, the breaking of a beloved toy is a tragedy, if it rains on the day when a picnic was planned one would think the sun could never shine for him again. If a mother or nurse leaves him while he is awake, he has been most treacherously betrayed. In fact, much early education has as its one goal the teaching of the little egotist to see himself in somewhat truer relation to his world. More or less successfully, each of us has had to learn this lesson; but it is almost never fully understood. To our last days there is still a trace of that childish egotism in us---sometimes so very much more than a trace that an adult suffers, resents, sulks, and complains in a way only too reminiscent of the nursery.

There is no success which does not entail a relationship between the individual and others. (That artist who "works only to please himself" is a chimera, as mythical a beast as the hippogriff.) Since that is so, there will be occasions on which it is immensely important for us to see ourselves clearly, and in scale with those around us. Each of us at some time is in a position to have to say to himself "Here am I; here is the work I do; here are those I hope to help and please by this work." Imagination can help us to stand back and see that relationship in perspective, can analyze its parts and suggest to us the full scope of what we have undertaken.

The infantile adult can never see himself at one remove; even less can he see his work or the object he has made quite as it is, undistorted by the overestimation of personal pride, or the underestimation of humility and fear. Consequently he is never in a position to know just where his contribution does go in the scheme of his world, and is at the mercy of the reports of friends or strangers. Even here he is bewildered; however plain the words may be, however just the estimate which is given him, he will not hear exactly what is said because he cannot bring to the moment his undivided and unemotional attention. His intense preoccupation with his own hopes and desires spoils him as a recording instrument. He cannot benefit by good advice or sound criticism; nor, on the other hand, can he know when such advice is mistaken, and the criticism not expert. By looking, in imagination, first at himself, then at the work he wants to do, then at the audience to whom he hopes to appeal; and, finally, by bringing all these elements into relation with each other, he could keep his courage from being undermined, his mind unconfused by conflicting advice, his estimate of his performance just.

Now, to identify ourselves too long with work we do is a bad mistake, and a mistake through which we can be hurt and hampered. The past few years have taught us much about the folly of so identifying ourselves with our children that they are rendered incapable of leading independent lives. The mother who clings to her adult (or even adolescent) child, suffering with him, making his decisions, undergoing humiliation on his account, unable to live her own life fully if he is not leading the sort of life she covets for him, meddling with his affairs, dictating his professional and social interests, is no longer looked upon as the sum of maternal love and wisdom.

While we may not always practice as wisely as we should, few men and women today consider the complete identification of themselves with their children as either praiseworthy or desirable. We have to that extent learned perspective about one of the most fundamental relations of life. We know that our work as parents is to do all in our power to equip the child to live a happy, healthy adult life, to put up no unnecessary barriers before his independent activities, to leave him free to select his friends and to form his own judgments as soon as possible. What is more, we know that it is desirable that every adult, whether parent or child, should have his own interests, and that only the possession of such interests will guarantee that no unwholesome interference with the life of another will take place. Further, no one believes for a moment that because a saner understanding of a parent's functions is replacing the old dictatorship, which was tyrannical even when it was motivated by deep affection, the love between mother or father and child is in any way decreasing.

The analogy of any finished piece of work with a child is very close: each has to be carried, cherished, nourished as part of one's very self during the early stages. But with full growth there comes a time when each should have its independent identity.

If we intend to get all we can from living, we must learn when to go on from one task to the next. Even the most productive of us could contribute more than be does; our output is about halved because we do not learn to separate ourselves from the things that are done and put our energy into the work which is ahead. Instead we turn and watch the fortunes of what we have lately been engrossed in. To some extent this is inevitable; we need to know the history and fortunes of our finished work in so far as we can learn anything valuable from them. But here is a place where the average man can learn from the genius. Abundance, as Edith Wharton has said, is the sign of the true vocation; and that is so in any branch of life. Your true genius---whether a Leonardo, a Dickens, a Napoleon, an

Edison---is always going on. Versatility and abundance are not, as we are sometimes told, the signs of the mediocre workman.

When they are present in a mediocre man, they are, on the contrary, the very things he has in common with the great men of his profession.

So accustomed are we to doing a piece of work, and then standing still to contemplate what happens to it, that we constantly wonder at those who do not make the same error. We even, erroneously, believe that they must "drive themselves" relentlessly in order to accomplish what they manage to do. Now, nothing of the sort is true---or it is not necessarily true. What has happened is that the time, the energy, the attention which in lesser men goes into waiting for approval, listening to comments, wondering whether some item or other might have been better done, is going forward and opening up new paths. It is not at all that the healthfully prolific men and women are complacent, or oblivious to real criticism; they know that if anything pertinent is said they will hear it. Experience has taught them that we are never deaf to what truly concerns us. What they have learned is not to wait to hear comment; and so their lives are twice as full and satisfactory as those of us who cannot learn when to let the results of our thought and labor, our mental offspring, go out to lead their own lives.

Imagination can bring us to understand how such sane workers operate, and suggest ways in which we can imitate them.

Chapter 10 - On Codes and Standards

BUT what if you must have approval and acquiescence in one phase of your work before you go on to the next? What if your work is contributory to a group effort? That is, of course, more complicated, but imagination can still come to your aid. It can show you where you stand in the chain of causes which go to bring about a certain result, and thus teach you to be patient during the time when your work is being considered, to hold yourself in a state of balance until the verdict is passed.

Then, if it is adverse---as it occasionally must be---you can do one of two things: tackle the same problem from a new angle, hoping this time to reach a good working basis with your co-workers, or you must put your reasons for believing that your original idea is good in such a way as to show that you are not defending it simply out of a sense of outraged proprietorship.

The only way to do this successfully is to have a well-thought-out set of standards drawn up for each type of work that you do, and in advance. If you wait till any one item is finished you may find yourself reasoning after the fact, defending the fact accomplished, and perhaps blinding yourself to real insufficiencies in it.

Here again we call on imagination. If you were to envisage the best possible example of the work you are about to undertake, what would it be? Find the best example of similar work that you can. What qualifications does it have? Which ones are vitally necessary? Which were added by the originator of that example? With this analysis in hand, draw up a set of standards for your own use, putting down first those things which are absolutely necessary if you are to succeed at all; next those which are desirable if it is possible to include them; last, but most important to your personal success, those things which are your own contribution.

Now, before getting to work, drop your own point of view and see your prospective task from the position of your audience, of the "ultimate consumer." Who is to benefit by the activity? Who, if you are a creative worker, is your audience? Who, if you are selling an article, is your predestined customer? If you were in his shoes, what would you like to see included in the offering? If you can imaginatively enter into the state of mind of those through whom you hope to attain your success, you can frequently add just those elements which will make your work irresistible.

(Take a very prosaic instance with which we are all familiar, the simple matter of kitchen equipment. Why do you suppose that for years most stoves, sinks, laundry tubs, continued to be made so low that the women who worked at them tired quickly from the abnormal positions they were forced to take? There was no good reason; but the moment some inspired person thought not merely how all such things were already being made, not merely of selling an adequate object, but of the comfort of those who were to use his product when sold, a revolution in kitchen equipment came about. Often such an improvement is staring us in the face; an obvious small change can be made which will bring an article, which we all buy in its unsatisfactory form simply because no better one is offered, out of its traditional shape into a form which will have, besides the element of novelty, that of greater convenience or usefulness.

That change will only be made by the person who is imaginative about his work, who can not only analyze the present form of an object into its essential parts, but who can imaginatively enter the life of the person who is to use it later.) Oddly enough, it is more often the creative worker who fails to expand the standards for his work by considering the half-formulated desires of his audience. Part of his intention, at least, must be to convey an idea or an aesthetic emotion to others, and he fails if he does not do so. It is true that to have a constant gnawing fear that you are not pleasing others has a bad effect on work. It is true that if you look exclusively to please others what you do will seldom be worth doing; but if your idea of success includes recognition, then the more you can learn imaginatively of your audience the better. If, knowing their tastes, you can give them not only what they want but something much better than they, being nonprofessionals, could imagine, you are sure of your success.

Having taken all these things into consideration, having formulated as clearly as possible the ideal towards which your own work should tend, before launching it into the world you should check it against a set of questions which arise logically from the possession of well-defined standards. Each line of activity will have a different set, each individual worker will alter the emphasis, or have his own idea of the proper order for these critical questions, but roughly the finished work should be measured in somewhat this way:

Is what I have done as good as the best in its field? Has it everything necessary for all ordinary purposes?

Have I added any special values by way of an original contribution?

Have I made it as attractive and convenient as possible for those who are its logical users? (Or audience, or clients.)

Have I considered whether there is another group to which it might also be made to appeal?

What more can I do before I release it from myself and send it out to make its own way?

(Try reading these questions in two ways: as referring to an item of commerce; as an attitude towards a daily task.)

The artist will necessarily have a different set of questions, although they will be cognate with those above. As an example, one of our best poets asks herself these questions:

Have I conveyed what I thought?

Have I conveyed what I felt?

Is it as clear as I can make it?

Is it as distinguished or beautiful as its matter permits?

Again, if you are one of a group of workers, imagination can help you in still another way, by showing you where you stand in relation to those around you. When you have seen this you can work out a code for yourself which will remove many of the irritations and dissatisfactions of your daily work. Have you ever been amused and enlightened by seeing a familiar room from the top of a stepladder; or, in mirrors set at angles to each other, seen yourself as objectively for a second or two as anyone else in the room? It is that effect you should try for in imagination. If you can see yourself and your fellow workers as impersonally as men on a chessboard, you can often find what it is that you are not doing, or what you are doing imperfectly, and move to correct the bad practice.

Many of those who believe themselves overworked are doing less than they should ideally do, and could do easily if they saw what is expected of them with imagination instead of anxiety. Often the excess work is something which they have almost officiously undertaken, many times from a real sense of duty and obligation. No large office is without one example of this type who is its reductio ad absurdum, the panicky job-grabber: from fear lest he, or, usually, she might possibly be considered as not doing all that is expected, or might be considered unnecessary to the organization, he gets a hundred small details in his hands, with the result that he is overworked, performance is not perfect, time is lost, and others who might be well occupied have time to idle and lose interest. If such a worker could see his position in perspective he could do more of the work he was really engaged for, do it better, and do it with less sense of strain and fatigue.

Those executives and administrators who continually do far more than they can without incurring fatigue and irritability are frequently pandering to their own self importance and conceit, although usually they would reject the charge with wrath.

They are certainly allowing the Will to Fail to operate in their lives. It is good to extend one's normal activity till its capacity is reached---and that is far oftener much more than we habitually do rather than less---but the tasks taken on thereafter are the first steps towards failure---towards that trouble, beloved of Americans, the "nervous breakdown."

When you have found your function, perform it very fully, but do not overstep it except in emergencies. In most large enterprises, or joint enterprises, there is---or should be---some one person whose decisions are final. Sometimes each member of a partnership has the power of command or veto for one aspect of the work. Often these decisions are given after the opinions of all have been canvassed, or suggestions invited. Right here comes the necessity for a code: if the decision goes against you or your suggestion, abandon your own idea and cooperate in the decision whole heartedly. If you feel that a truly grave mistake is being made, take a few hours to draw up the situation as you see it, show how you think the new decision will alter matters, why you think it is a mistake, or why an alternative plan should be adopted.

Try to be as fair about this as you can. Often we think an alternative plan precious because, and only because, it is our own. "Pride of authorship" comes in.

Many of those who believe they have given up their own ideas and are working along other lines will unconsciously go on obstructing and objecting, holding up the work, trying to defeat its ends. The trouble here is that this obstructionism is often unconscious; but the way to escape the danger is to realize it as a possibility, and to look at yourself and your attitude scrupulously to be sure you are not putting up unnecessary hazards, doing your share of the new program slowly or indifferently---trying to bring about a failure, since your plan was ignored or modified.

If, on the other hand, you are the one whose decisions must be accepted, you will save yourself trouble later by watching the initial stages of the work to be sure that some such unconscious sabotage is not going on. A quick challenge to the troublesome person whose feelings have been hurt will sometimes whip a whole program into shape which might otherwise fail. And by such watching you can see that each is doing the work assigned to him.

A little imaginative overseeing of a staff or partnership in the early stages of any activity will often result in clearing up a disorder of long standing.

Perhaps, however, you are really miscast, and your usefulness would be on, say, the planning end of an enterprise rather than the executive, where you are placed. In that case, your problem is to bring your talents to the attention of your superior officers with as little crowding and bustling as possible. Learn to write clear, short, definite memoranda and present them to your immediate superior until you are perfectly certain that he will never act upon them, in no other circumstances are you justified in going over his head. Try also to be willing to see your work and suggestions acted upon without receiving immediate acknowledgment that the ideas originated with you. This frequently happens in a large organization, and to sulk or stand out for having your rights recognized in every case will only cancel the advance you might have been able to make. If your good idea is one of a series and not a flash in the pan, you can be sure your caliber will eventually make itself felt. If not, the organization is a bad one for you, and you should set about finding a better connection as soon as possible.

Partnerships, and particularly the universal partnership of husband and wife, are almost always individual cases. In general the rule should be, try never to assume what is the normal function of the other partner until you have almost indisputable evidence that if you do not do so some vital balance will be destroyed. Often to do one's own part fully and well is enough to call out the complementary activities of the other. In any partnership, once you are sure that you are doing your own part, if there is still some obvious weakness to correct it can usually be talked over, the reason for it found, and its correction arranged. Occasionally this cannot be done. Only those who are in such a relation know when it is impossible to talk over any matter because of an oversensitiveness or blindness in the other partner. In such cases, assume as much of the overlooked responsibility as you can discharge well, but no more. There is always the possibility of sudden illumination, of belated growth, which will be endangered if you take upon yourself more than you should. But notice that where you must do work not your own, assume these responsibilities; see that you do not allow them to be thrust upon you. What you undertake open-eyed will seldom be made later a cause of martyrdom and sullenness.

When once you have seen imaginatively what your scope should be, both as an individual and as a member of a group, a society, or a partnership you are ready to teach, discipline and exercise yourself till you reach your state of maximum effectiveness.

Chapter 11 - Twelve Disciplines

ONE

THERE are dozens of small ways by which we can make our minds both keener and more flexible---two qualities peculiarly necessary for those who intend to live successfully. We all succumb too easily to the temptation to find a routine which works out so that we get our day's tasks done with a minimum of effort and conscious attention; a fact which might have no unfortunate effects on us at all if we used the time we save by our routines to good purpose. But the cold truth is that we do nothing of the sort. We apply the routine-observing tendency to our whole lives, growing mentally and spiritually more flaccid, more timorous, less experimental with every day we spend supported by the rigidity of habit.

Habit takes care of most of our ordinary activities; we get through our work by using only that part of our intellect which has been trained to consider the work's specific problems (often trained painfully and protesting); when we meet a novel thought or situation, we fall back on an analogy and act according to the prejudice or emotion which that arouses in us. Even those of us who rather solemnly undertake programs of self-improvement seldom use more than one set of mental muscles, gathering a number of facts about this subject or that, and considering ourselves "improved" if we learn something about the religions of India, or the work of Charles Dickens, or the birds of Southern California.

This would be harmless enough if it were not for the complacency which attends it.

Fact gathering is one activity of the intellect; and where a little training in independent judgment has accompanied or preceded it, so that correct conclusions concerning the facts are independently reached, it is a valuable one. But such programs alone do not exercise the mind to its fullest extent, to make an instantaneously useful tool of it, or give one the power to call on all its resources at will.

Even those who think of themselves as extraordinarily hard workers are not in the state of mental training, usually, which allows them to get the most from their lives.

One great reason is pointed out over and over by Dr. Alexis Carrel in his book Man, the Unknown: the benefits of civilization are not unmixed blessings. We are no longer called on to meet the extremes of heat and cold, for instance, to go through alternate periods of plenty and scarcity of food; universal lighting turns night into day everywhere, and the newspapers and radio entertain us so that we seldom look to ourselves for our own resources. Healthy man has a great capacity for adaption, and, says Dr. Carrel, "the exercise of the adaptive functions appears to be indispensable to the optimum development of man." We have allowed ourselves to soften, to abandon our ingenuity, to escape responsibility whenever possible, till we grow to fear and abhor the very word "discipline."

Yet discipline is undergoing restraint in order to develop the qualities necessary for a full life. Mental discipline should connote the equivalent in the sphere of the mind which the athlete undertakes for perfecting his body. We should first take stock of our minds; and then set to work on them to strengthen them here, make them more flexible there, stretch them somewhat, teach them to be more exact---in short, put them through their paces so that we get the maximum use and advantage from them.

In order to do so, we must learn to be arbitrary with ourselves---by no means an easy matter for a generation which has not only been softened by material conveniences, but has been given the dubious benefit of being allowed to "psychologize" about itself day in and day out. Some of us dread and dislike restraint, even when self imposed for a sound purpose, to such an extent that we live our lives between habit and impulse under the impression that only so can we be wholly free. But "Freedom," says Aristotle, "is obedience to self-formulated rules," and the definition holds as good today as two thousand years ago.

We must work to get back tone and muscle into our lives until it is possible to stop one activity and turn to another, varying the approach, stroke, strength behind the effort, and so on, with as much agility and deftness as a skillful tennis player uses to meet the shifting play of a good opponent. If we could know each day just the necessities we should be called on to meet, we could prepare ourselves in advance, and flexibility and ingenuity would be uncalled for. Since that does not happen, we must get ourselves into training to meet the infinite calls on us, instead of, as we usually do, discharging easily only one or two matters which are natively congenial to us, and getting through the others awkwardly, blindly.

The disciplines suggested here are drawn from all over the world. Readers of philosophy and religion will find procedures they have met before, recommended by the wise men of many countries: there are disciplines from India and Spain, from Greece and China---and from any girl's finishing school! Some of them are common to every country which teaches any kind of mental or spiritual discipline, such as that of observing set periods of silence. None of them is "arbitrary" in the sense of "pointless"; each develops or strengthens a faculty of the mind which should be kept in good condition if a life is to be led purposefully and under one's own control.

Not all of them will be equally valuable to all cases; but before rejecting any one of them examine yourself to discover if you are not possibly throwing it aside simply because it does ask you to put a little more restraint on yourself than you find pleasurable. Most of them will be difficult at some stage, attended by something in the mental realm like the stiffness and soreness which follow using a new muscle in athletic training. But you can exercise muscle only by submitting it to some sort of resistance; you must feel at least slightly uncomfortable to have the assurance that your exercise is doing the work you are asking of it. So, in following these mental exercises, unless there is some discomfort from observing each one fully, unless there is some protest arising from interrupted habits and novel ways of action, it may be that the discipline in question is not one that you really need. Replace it, in that case, with another which calls on you for some endurance and effort.

TWO

The Twelve Disciplines

1.

The first exercise is to spend an hour every day without saying anything except in answer to direct questions. This should be done in the midst of your usual group, and without giving anyone the impression that you are sulking or suffering from a bad headache. Present as ordinary an appearance as possible; simply do not speak.

Answer questions just to their limit, aid no further; give a full and adequate answer, but do not continue with volunteered remarks which are suggested by the answer or question, and do not attempt in any way to draw another question from your interlocutor. Oddly enough, this is a difficult discipline for even a normally taciturn person. We are all so used to breaking into speech wherever we meet one another, merely in order to give evidence of our friendliness and accessibility, that we talk almost constantly whenever there is an opportunity.

This discipline is found in almost every country which is the home of a genuinely old religion. It is of immense value, and productive of many different results. Probably no two experimenters ever have identical reactions to this practice; they will vary according to temperaments. One thing which soon becomes apparent to many, for instance, is that we seldom say exactly what we mean at our first attempt. We rush into speech, see by the expression on another's face that we have not made ourselves entirely clear, or have misspoken in some way, and try again. This likewise may not make our intention understood; we try again. We pause a moment, think the matter over, issue a clearer statement. But in the meanwhile there are those three earlier attempts to express ourselves still remaining in our hearers' minds, beclouding the issue.

One man, reporting on this experiment, said that he seemed at first not to be there at all. Then there was a period when he felt that he, in his silence, filled the whole room and had the experience of seeing it all impersonally. As long as he talked, wherever he stood was, naturally, the center of his scene; silent, the group "composed" with a different emphasis. When his hour was over he saw himself sometimes in the center, sometimes on the circumference, occasionally entirely outside the interests around him.

Another man recorded that when his silence began to make itself felt the friends he was with acted most illuminatingly. Not quite aware what made the occasion unusual, two of them were definitely ill at ease. One thereupon became extremely ingratiating, a second truculent and then downright hostile, arriving at the point of charging his silent friend with feeling "superior" just as the hour was up and speech could be resumed. A third man, heretofore the quietest of the group of friends, turned extremely talkative, as though to retrieve a balance he felt endangered, relapsing into silence when the observer began to talk naturally again.

A woman reported, with much amusement, that she had never had such a personal success in her life as during the hour she sat silent and smiling at a party. Her silence seemed to act as a magnet and a challenge in a way her gaiety had never done.

All experimenters, however, agreed on one matter: while the silence lasted a sense of mastery grew in them. When they resumed speech it was with the sense of using speech definitely and purposefully, and always with the knowledge that the resort of silence could be found at Meredith which she said she had never fully understood.

One concluded her report with a sentence from before: "It is the silence of the god we fear, not his wrath; Silence is the unbearable repartee."

2.

Learn to think for half-an-hour a day exclusively on one subject. Simple as this sounds, it is at first ludicrously hard to do. The novice should begin by thinking on his solitary subject for five minutes a day at first, increasing the period daily till the half hour has been attained. To begin with, a concrete object should be chosen: a flower, a bottle of ink, a scarf. Do not have it before you; build it up in your mind. With a flower, for instance, describe it to yourself as each of the senses would report it.

When that is done, go on to how it grows and where; what it symbolizes, if anything; what uses are made of it. From this simple beginning, work up to considering a concrete problem, and, finally, to an abstraction. Start with subjects which really interest you, but when you have taught your mind not to wander even for a moment, begin choosing a subject by pointing your finger at random on a newspaper or the page of a book, and think on the first idea suggested by the lines you have touched.

You will find it very revealing to start this exercise with a pencil and pad, and to make a slight check on the paper whenever you find your attention slipping. If you are really quick to realize when your mind has begun to wander, you will find your paper very full for the first few days. Fortunately, improvement in this is fairly rapid.

At the end of a week in some cases, at the end of a month even in refractory ones, the pad will be found nearly blank at the end of your half-hour. The value of this exercise must be obvious to anyone who hopes to engage in original work, or to introduce new procedures of any sort. At first it is wise to practice this when alone; but eventually you should be able to do it even in the midst of distractions, such as when traveling to and from work.

(Note carefully that the recommendation is not to hold one's mind immobile on one object, as in some Indian disciplines or in the Christian process called "recollection." You are to think about one subject only; no more than that. The other practice induces a slightly hypnoidal state, and is not suitable to our purposes here.) This, of course, is simply the "application" and "concentration" which was preached to every one of us in our school days, it is very revealing, none the less, to see how imperfectly we learned that lesson then or at any subsequent time! Once it is learned, it is of immense benefit. Anyone who is capable of it, for instance, can pick up a foreign language in very short order. The accent may be barbarous, unless one has learned phonetics early, but books and newspapers can be easily read, and enough of a vocabulary to get around in the strange land can be acquired in less than a month.

Moreover, in any competitive performance, the one who has trained himself to think steadily, without deflection, will arrive at his conclusion first. But the advantages of this are too obvious to need emphasizing further.

3.

Write a letter without once using the following words: I, me, my, mine. Make it smooth and keep it interesting. If the recipient of the letter notices that there is something odd about it, the exercise has failed.

This practice, and others like it, again allows us to see ourselves in perspective. In order to write a good letter of the sort, it is necessary to turn the mind outward, to give up for a while the preoccupations and obsessions with our own affairs. We come back to our own lives refreshed.

4.

Talk for fifteen minutes a day without using I, me, my, mine.

5.

Write a letter in a "successful" or placid tone. No actual misstatements are allowed.

No posing as successful, no lying. Simply look for aspects or activities which can be honestly reported in this way and confine you letter to them. Indicate by the letter's tone that you are, at the moment of writing, not discouraged in any way.

There is a double purpose here. First, it is a simple way of turning from a negative and discouraging attitude towards a positive and healthy one. However unpromising the prospect for finding enough good items for a letter may appear at first, one soon discovers that a number of matters are going smoothly and well, but that they have been ignored while one centers on disappointment and frustration. Second, and more important, such a letter as this, sent to almost every correspondent you have, will remove one great stumbling-block to the successful conduct of your affairs.

Letter writing is a task we usually tuck into an odd corner of our day. When we have nothing to do and feel listless, bored, tired or depressed, we take pen in hand and write to our dear ones! We send low-spirited, unhappy notes about, and reap the natural consequences: consolatory or sympathetic letters come in answer. Sometimes they come when we are feeling fairly well, or in really high spirits; but it is a heroic character who can resist the chance to feel sorry for himself. We have the choice, reading these answers which we have invited, of slipping back into the mood of martyrdom and self-pity, or of feeling distinctly silly. It is far more dramatic to feel sad again than to feel silly; so we go on in our vicious circle, and send the latest bad news when we write again. A complete holiday from self-pity and depressions is necessary to success.

6.

And this exercise comes directly from all the finishing schools for young ladies that ever existed: pause on the threshold of any crowded room you are to enter, and consider for a moment your relation to those who are in it Many a retiring and quiet woman can thank this small item of her school training for her ability to handle competently situations which seem, as though they would be embarrassing and exacting for anyone so sheltered. It was for years (and may be still, for all I know) the custom to teach young girls to stop just a moment at the door of the room they were entering until they had found their hostess, and then the guest of honor. (Failing such guest, the oldest person in the room was to be singled out.) Then the room was entered, the young guest going, as soon as her hostess was free, straight to her to be welcomed and to "make her manners." She then watched for the first opportunity to speak for a few minutes to the guest of honor; and not until she had discharged these obligations was she free to follow any other plans or inclinations of her own. The girl who thoroughly learned this lesson learned something which is invaluable to everyone: to size up a roomful of people at a glance, discover what it holds, first in the way of obligation and then in the way of companionship or one's own interests.

There is a kind of nonsensical notion abroad today that to take such conscious forethought about any occasion is to be a hypocrite or a snob, that there is some virtue in rushing pell-mell into any situation, snatching what offers itself without difficulty, and foregoing the rest. There is no danger that you will really be acting "artificially" if you give yourself a moment to foresee the various possibilities and relationships in the occasion you are about to live through. You will simply have taken care not to be stampeded into doing something uncongenial to you, of getting caught in a backwater of conversation which touches none of your real interests, or of running the risk of missing a chance to talk to a real friend, or someone whose conversation will bring you something of value. However consciously we plan our lives, there is still enough margin of the unforeseen and the unexpected to keep us from any danger of losing spontaneity, but the ideal is to have as much of our lives within our voluntary control as possible. Sometimes, with the best of intentions, we are not able to bring about what we want in that moment of anticipation; if we have taken the trouble to see all the possibilities before us, we can turn to a secondary interest easily, not missing every opportunity because we were disappointed in one.

7.

When the above exercise is learned or recaptured, go on to an old piece of advice from seventeenth century France: keep a new acquaintance talking about himself or herself without allowing him to become conscious of what you are doing. Turn back, at first, any courteous reciprocal questions in such a way that your auditor does not feel rebuffed. You will find a genuine interest rising in you for your companion; soon, if you are at all kindly or imaginative, you will find yourself engrossed. The last, lingering trace of self-consciousness will drop from you. It may be that you will not be asked about yourself. That makes no difference; at the very least you have learned a little more about how the world looks to another, and have extended your horizon.

If, on the other hand, you do talk of yourself in response to later questions, you will know just how much to say, what interests you have in common, whether you could ever find the friendship of that person desirable.

(Perhaps it needs to be said plainly that acting consciously need not mean acting coldly. Not a grain of real humanity is sacrificed by having the reins of action in one's own hands; rather the contrary. An outgoing effort is voluntarily undertaken and carried on; instead of being so totally engrossed in ourselves that we know nothing of the moods or interests of others except as they affect us, we escape by the pleasantest road from our restricting egotism. The other party to the experiment, far from being a victim of coldblooded planning, is for once assured of not being victimized by our blind selfishness.)

8.

The exact opposite of the above exercises, and infinitely harder to do with intention: Talk exclusively about yourself and your interests without complaining, boasting or (if possible) boring your companion. Make yourself and your activities as interesting as you can to the person to whom you are talking.

This is an excellent discipline for those who ordinarily talk too much about themselves. This reductio ad absurdum of their weakness brings them face to face with the ordeal which they are putting their friends through at every opportunity.

When concentrated talking about one's own interests is undertaken consciously, every sign of indifference, of boredom, of restiveness or impatience, of desire to introduce another topic of conversation which may escape us while we are neurotically self absorbed, is only too plainly seen. Both the exercise and the weakness will be abandoned gratefully after one or two occasions.

However, there are other things to be gained from this. It soon becomes apparent that talking about the trivial, the commonplace, the recurring incidents of one's life leads to certain ennui in our hearers. If, on the other hand, we have had genuinely interesting experiences, have been more imaginative in a situation than usual, are undertaking something new, we are likely to hold our audience. The conclusion that in that case perhaps we might profit by extending our interests, undertaking new adventures, or bringing more imagination to our everyday lives can hardly be escaped. We soon learn to discard a report of our latest attack of illness, the most recent exploit of our offspring, the remarkable intelligence of our pets, today's example of our bad luck, as opening gambits in adult conversation. If you are with someone who is still a slave to that kind of word-wasting, consciously introduce a subject of more depth or wider interest when it is your turn to speak. If you discover that he or she stubbornly resists all such invitations to better talk, you have a decision to make.

There may be, in spite of all limitations, such warmth, sweetness, genuine feeling in even a limited friend that one can under no circumstances think of abandoning the relationship. On the other hand, we sometimes discover, to our surprised dismay, that we have attached someone to ourselves for no better reason than that in his presence we can babble on about the trivialities of our lives, though there is no deep bond between us. To withdraw from that association as soon as is consistent without hurting the other party, to refuse to continue to waste your own energy and time, or connive in the wasting of his, is a plain obligation. If you have been guilty (as most of us have) of forming such an association-in-weakness, the first effort at correction should be to see whether you can not transform it into a genuine friendship, stimulating and strengthening; only when you must give up all hope of that should the relationship be dropped.

9.

The correction of the "I-mean," the "As-a-matter-of-fact" habit, takes cooperation. If you realize that you have picked up a verbal mannerism, call on the friend to whom you talk most fluently and emotionally. It is fairly easy to control such a mannerism in the presence of someone we hardly know, but in the heat of discourse the offending phrase will crop up in every other sentence. Tell the friend that you are saying "and so on," for instance, to the point of absurdity. Ask him to watch for it, and to hold up his hand without interrupting the conversation whenever he hears you use it. The talk which follows will be choppy, and there is likely for a while to be more laughter than conversation, but you will begin to get the habit in hand. Two or three sessions will entirely eradicate the phrase---except when you actually want to use it.

10.

Plan two hours of a day and live according to the plan.

If you are working by yourself as a free lance, any day will do. If not, choose a Sunday or holiday to experiment on. Make the schedule partly according to your usual habit, partly unlike it. As for instance:

7:308 Breakfast and newspaper

88:20 Mail

8:209:25 Arrange books according to subject matter

9:259:30 Telephone (if on weekday) for some appointment you have been putting off.

If Sunday or holiday, go out for a walk.

The complexity or diversity of the items has very little to do with this practice. The point is to turn from one activity to the next, not at the approximate minute of your schedule, but on the exact moment. If you are only halfway through the newspaper, that's very sad. But down it must go, and you open your mail---hitherto disregarded. If this is a day without an incoming mail, the twenty minutes go to letter writing. If you have time to spare, send a card or two, or make notes for another letter on another day. Wherever you are at 8:20 with your correspondence, you stop and turn to the arranging of books. One of your planned activities, at least, should promise a fair amount of interest to you. If it is not arranging books, then clipping articles from a magazine can replace it, or even straightening a room thoroughly.

The twin purposes of this discipline are, first, to give ourselves the experience of being under orders again, and, second, to demonstrate how badly we lose our sense of the time necessary to accomplish any stipulated activity. Every printer that ever lived, probably, has grumbled at an editor or make up man who wants to crowd too many letters on a line, complaining that "he must think we've got rubber type." Well, most of us think our days have rubber hours. Even those suburbanites who have learned by long experience that it is just seventeen minutes to a second from the shower-bath to the railroad station will nonchalantly plan to cram the work of half a day into a couple of hours after lunch. We expect time to be infinitely accommodating, we refuse to admit that it cannot be. But it is possible to learn---by planning, first, two hours of a day, then three, then four, and so on till we have planned and lived an effective, eight hour day (at the least) --- to use time to the best advantage. Rigid scheduling of a whole day is not always possible or even desirable, but a few days lived by timetable now and again will refresh our sense of the value of time and teach us what we can expect of ourselves when we do not waste it.

For those who need really stern warning about this: one psychiatrist, Dr. Paul Bousfeld, holds that the sure sign of the incurable egotist is that he never allows for the actual amount of time any given activity will take. Firmly, though unconsciously, believing that the world revolves around him, certain of his magical power to arrest the progress of the sun and the moon, he goes through life astonished at the refractoriness of Time in not meeting him halfway. He is always late to appointments, behind in his obligations, constantly assuming more work or accepting more invitations than he could keep if he were twins. He either learns the error of his ways or comes to a bad end.

11.

This is the most difficult of all. It will seem so arbitrary to many readers that they will not even try to apply it. It is arbitrary; that is its very essence. It is less necessary for those living in the midst of large families than for persons living alone, or those who are alone most of the time. Remembering the quotation given before from Dr. Cairel, arrange to put yourself into situations where you must act non-habitually, where you must adapt yourself. Members of the Army, the Navy, the priesthood, some societies, are constantly in a state of living under orders; and we recognize in them a resiliency that is absent from the characters of most men and women who live according to their own convenience. It is not easy to get this resiliency back into our lives, but it is a quality too valuable to be lost. If the following recommendation seems somewhat too dramatic, almost too ridiculous, be assured that the results will show the worth of the discipline.

On a number of slips of paper---twelve will do to start with---write instructions like these:

"Go twenty miles from home, using ordinary conveyance." (In other words, don't just get out a car or hire a taxi, if you can afford it, and drive somewhere. Take streetcars, buses, ferries, subways.)

"Go twelve hours without food."

"Go eat a meal in the unlikeliest place you can find." A restaurant in a totally foreign quarter of a city is good here. Asking for food at a farmhouse is better, if you are hardy enough to be so unconventional.

"Say nothing all day except in answer to questions."

"Stay up all night and work."

And this, by the way, is the most valuable order of them all. You must plan to work steadily and quietly, resisting every temptation to lie down for a few moments, but relaxing very slightly against the chair-back every hour or so, bracing yourself to your work again the moment lassitude threatens to overcome you. Only those who have actually done this realize that there are depths to our minds which we seldom plumb, accustomed as we are to succumb to the first attack of fatigue, or staying awake only so long as we have outer stimulation.

Seal these slips of paper in twelve envelopes, shuffle them thoroughly and put them in a drawer. Whenever you think of it, shuffle them again. Every other week, or on a given day of each month, pick one of the envelopes, open it, and perform your own command. It may be raining pitchforks on the day you command yourself to travel twenty miles by common carrier; nevertheless, unless your state of health absolutely forbids it, you go. If you are doing an intensive piece of work, one monthly exercise of this sort is enough. If not, the oftener you can be arbitrary with yourself---without turning into a restless jumping jack, it goes without saying---the better for your character eventually.

There need not be twelve different orders on your slips. If you can think of activities which are genuinely difficult for you to do, which go against the grain but which you yet know would be valuable training for you, include them. One young man of my acquaintance who was abnormally shy insisted to himself that he should get into conversation with at least three strangers daily. Any activity you choose should be both corrective and unusual, cutting abruptly across your usual routine.

12.

An alternative method is this: from time to time give yourself a day on which you say "Yes" to every request made of you which is at all reasonable. The more you tend to retire from society in your leisure, the more valuable this will be. You may find yourself invited to go sleigh riding in your twenty-four hours; you may be invited to change your job. The sleigh-ride should certainly be accepted, however much you may hate straw, thick blankets and cold weather. The job-changing, fortunately, can be submitted to examination, since it is only "reasonable" activities which you are to undertake without second thought. Don't be afraid nothing will occur on that day; it is astonishing how many small requests we can turn aside daily rather than interrupt our even course. The consequences may be wide-reaching, often educative, sometimes extremely advantageous. Nevertheless do not jump to the conclusion that because one day of the sort has brought so many interesting possibilities to light, every day should be led in that manner. On the contrary; to deny oneself an opportunity now and again is fully as illuminating, particularly for those who waste too much time in party-going, theaters, and so on. Such persons should plan to refuse many invitations, and spend the time in intensive self-cultivation.

On this system, work out other disciplines which are good for your individual case.

There are two ways of making them. First, become aware of some weakness or inadequate performance on your part; then decide, perhaps after experiment, whether the way to correct it is to set yourself to doing the exact opposite, or whether---as in curing the habit of talking too much about one's own interests---acting a ludicrous and overemphasized parody of the failing will be more effective.

Once you get the idea, you will find these disciplines not only helpful but genuinely amusing. In many cases they replace the rather haphazard puzzle-solving activities which call on somewhat the same capacities. In matching your wits against yourself you take on the shrewdest and wiliest antagonist you can have, and consequently a victorious outcome in this duel of wits brings a great feeling of triumph. At last, when one is in training, one can call at will on any of the mental traits which have been strengthened or exercised in these ways and find that it performs exactly and quickly.

But, as yon begin to take pleasure in these exercises, remind yourself that they are means, not ends. In getting control of your mind you are not yet using it officially, so to speak. You are still in your probationary period. Have you ever met one of those health-seekers who eat just so many ounces of food per day, walk just so many miles or play just so many games of handball, sit in the sun or under a sun lamp just so many minutes---and then lead the dullest of personal lives? He has made himself into a magnificently healthy creature---for no purpose whatsoever. You are training your mind in order to engage it in definite activity, so do not put off too long the matter of getting at your original plans.

THREE

Still considering what aids we can find to successful living, but now in the way of direct support for ourselves, there are various ways in which we can make the process smoother. One of the best is to follow the suggestion of Franklin, in his Autobiography, and to check daily on our progress by means of a small, specially prepared notebook. Franklin himself drew up a list of thirteen Virtues, and under each wrote a maxim embodying the sense of that virtue to his mind. For instance, under Temperance he wrote "Eat not to dullness; drink not to elevation"; under Silence: "Speak not but what may benefit others or yourself; avoid trifling conversation"; and so went on, through Order, Resolution, Frugality and the rest. It is hardly possible to draw up a better set, but---and perhaps it is one more sign of the softening of the race---for most purposes the six matters which we find most troublesome will seem quite enough for our present. Each will have his own set of faults to be corrected.

But let us say, for instance, that you decide you could do more work if you would; that you are shy, that you take too long to make up your mind; that you talk too much (and timidity and talkativeness are by no means mutually exclusive vices); that you eat at odd hours or the wrong things; that you sleep too long (or not enough). Your notebook page should look like this:

The checks represent your estimate of the number of times you successfully resisted the temptation to act in the unsatisfactory way. As you find yourself able to fill any of the squares of your notebook each day---in other words, when you have eradicated the trouble-making fault---you can retire that classification and replace it with another which you may have noticed. If you soon outgrow the need of the notebook, splendid.

It can be kept in a convenient drawer, though, as a reminder.

	S	M	T	W	T	F	S
Work	•						
Courage							
Decision	•						
Speech	•						
Meals	•						
Sleep							

Then there is the matter of getting into the day. Those who wake fully each morning would find it hard to believe how many of their fellows suffer from not being fully in command of their faculties in the morning. If you belong to the latter crew, don't hesitate to imitate the Katherine Mansfield hero who woke, opened his eyes, and saw the sign he had put up for himself: "Get out of bed at once."

What is more, if you know---as so many of us do---that at midnight you have a genuine inspiration which your morning's prosaic mood leads you to disregard, write yourself a note about it. Be pretty firm about the matter; put it sharply. Say to yourself, in writing, "You're an idiot if you don't at least see whether Macy's would like that idea. Make an appointment today!" Often nothing more is needed to make the prosy, unimaginative daylight mood break up and allow the intenser one to return.

One of the most famous men in America constantly sends himself postcards, and occasionally notes. He explained the card-sending as being his way of relieving his memory of unnecessary details. In his pocket he carries a few postals addressed to his office. I was with him one threatening day when he looked out the restaurant window, drew a card from his pocket and wrote on it. Then he threw it across the table to me with a grin. It was addressed to himself at his office, and said "Put your raincoat with your hat." At the office he had other cards addressed to himself at home.

Rewarding oneself for successful work---even in addition to the success---is another way of promoting proper action. If you get yourself some small luxury when, and only when, your notebook shows a week of satisfactory marks, you may go to slightly more trouble to turn away from your faults.

Get into the habit of being both strict and friendly toward yourself: demand a certain standard of performance; approve of yourself, even reward yourself, if you attain it.

Far too often we pursue just the wrong tactics. When we should be acting we indulge or excuse ourselves for inactivity we then upbraid and punish ourselves ruthlessly and futilely. The scolding is futile because we somehow feel that, if we have been severe and cutting to ourselves, we have in some way atoned for the fault of non performance. We have not, of course. We have not done what we planned, and we have discouraged and hurt ourselves into the bargain.

Chapter 12 - And The Best of Luck!

SUMMING up, then, we have as the first tenet of success: Act as if it were impossible to fail.

Beginning to put this into practice, we discover that the first demand upon us is that we should reclaim as much as possible of the energy which now goes into reverie or into time-killing, and devote it to purposeful activity, to action toward an end. We act by ignoring all memories or apprehensions of failure, by refusing to attach importance to temporary discomfort or past pain. We learn not to court frustration by using an attitude or tone which leaves any opportunity for rebuff or non-cooperation. We exercise our minds in trial performances in order to have them fully under our control when the occasion to use them in an expert way arises. With the imagination we painlessly explore all the possible reaches of our lives and constantly provide ourselves with projects of future interests to such an extent that we shall not fall back into day dreaming.

We deliberately make for ourselves an invigorating mental climate, and in this atmosphere, freed of doubts and anxieties, we act.

In the last few chapters we have been considering these facets of successful action one by one. Now it must be remembered that, however correct and suggestive such detailed considerations may be, they suffer badly in one manner: their tempo, so to speak, has had to be altered in order to show them minutely.

A slow-motion picture of ballplayers in action, of golfers, of a tennis match, is sometimes of inestimable value to these who are learning to play. The muscular effort behind a sudden dexterous turn of the body, in its normal tempo far too quick for the eye to catch, is shown in the retarded film in all its subtlety. But we gain our insight into the technique of difficult plays by losing sight, for the moment, of another aspect.

You will remember how, in such pictures, the player glides languorously through the air, the ball curves slowly towards the racquet, touches it with a soft impact and slides slowly away again. Illuminating as these pictures are, they are also always irresistibly comic: the leap, the crack, the rapidity of the game as we know it is gone, replaced by a twilit, dreaming gentleness.

Now, to consider the technique of success in these pages, we have had to sacrifice pace to analysis in just this way. The actual tempo of success, while it should not have the nervousness or strain that is almost inevitable in a competitive contest, is quicker, smoother, more brisk than any book analyzing it can ever show. There is a delightful conciseness in successful action. "I know I'm doing a good picture if I'm painting just as fast as I can move," a great artist said to a group of friends recently.

"The minute I dabble I know I'm stalling, that there's something I'm not seeing right; when I'm right it's almost like play."

There is undoubtedly something game-like about pertinent activity: those distressful clichés of a few years ago, "the advertising game," "the engineering game," "the restaurant game," had some excuse in reality. The vocabulary of men who are successful in the sense that they have amassed huge fortunes abounds in terms taken over from the jargon of sports: "A fast one," "Out of bounds," and so on. And however unlike the big business ambition of such a man one's own personal idea of success may be, there is something to be deduced from the frequency of recreation terms when stories of success are in question. Purposeful action seems quicker, clearer more straightforward and enjoyable than any other. In reality, you may be working more slowly and carefully than ordinarily; still, the fact that there is no confusion of issues, no part of your mind off woolgathering as you move, gives an unmistakable "tone" to activities which are being carried on in the proper way.

It is just this tone that you are setting yourself to recapture by imagination when you remember the mood of an earlier success. Once you have found it in the past, made use of it for present action, and noted the similarity in pace which results, you will soon be able to strike the right rhythm without the elaborate preliminary imaginative activity. Further, this rhythm sometimes crops out unexpectedly, in the middle of unimportant events; it is a promise that, if you can get away and at work, you will find yourself "in vein." So you will come to recognize its onset and be able to turn it to your advantage.

This feeling of pace, or tone, or rhythm---it represents itself differently to differing temperaments---will be your evidence that you are headed the right way. This is no recommendation to hasten your physical action in working. That may or may not come to pass. Very often it does; in other cases undue haste has been one of the contributions of the Will to Fail, which, aping the decisiveness of authoritative motion, allowed several essentials to good work to be overlooked or skimped.

It is not so much any real briskness that is being considered here as it is the fact that unimpeded movement in a forward direction is pleasant and rhythmical, movement which goes unwaveringly towards success.

Let us, for another *reductio ad absurdum*, consider one great class of successes, of which almost everyone has had some personal experience, or at the very least has met in the lives of those about him: the state called the courage of desperation.

In the most extreme cases, this courage arises because some catastrophe or series of misfortunes has completely wiped out every alternative to success. "He has nothing to lose," we say of one in this situation. Very well, then; he acts with a directness and daring which he could not ordinarily command. So often that it has become a matter of legend for us, this action is attended with overwhelming success. If you will remember the third victim of the Will to Fail in an earlier chapter, you will recall that he had made a state of desperation into a superstitious prerequisite to accomplishment. Quite misreading the situation, he came to believe that the prospect of utter vanquishment would, each time, cause Fate to relent. What he entirely overlooked was that when he had reached such straits that he dared not fail he invariably acted as he should always act: as if it were impossible to fail. Without exception in this state he succeeded. Inextricably involved in the meshes of his bad and emotional thinking, he invited failure as the only way to spur himself to effort. To his acquaintances he inevitably recalled the crazy hero of world-wide fame, the man who hit himself on the head with a hammer because it felt so good when he stopped.

It was and is all very serious to him.

But remove the absurdity from these examples of the courage of desperation, and we have the sense. Desperation does cut off one alternative. But desperation is not needed, is not the only tool which will cut away the possibility of failure. Imagination will do the work even better and more neatly. And we are left with Courage facing in-the-right-direction.

Courage facing in the right direction is the sine qua non of success. It is to reach that stage that we put ourselves through exercises in flexibility and restraint, learn to turn imagination away from apprehension and into useful channels, determine to act wisely in minor matters in order to store up courage for the major issues of our lives.

We use our heads to get the greatest good from our gifts and abilities, refusing ourselves the weakening privileges of dreaming, avoiding responsibilities, following the line of least resistance, acting childishly.

Success, for any sane adult, is exactly equivalent to doing one's best. What that best may be, what its farthest reaches may include, we can discover only by freeing ourselves completely from the Will to Fail.

Becoming A Writer
Originally published 1934

In Introduction

For most of my adult life I have been engaged in the writing, the editing, or the criticizing of fiction. I took, and I still take, the writing of fiction seriously. The importance of novels and short stories in our society is great. Fiction supplies the only philosophy that many readers know; it establishes their ethical, social, and material standards; it confirms them in their prejudices or opens their minds to a wider world. The influence of any widely read book can hardly be overestimated. If it is sensational, shoddy, or vulgar our lives are the poorer for the cheap ideals which it sets in circulation; if, as so rarely happens, it is a thoroughly good book, honestly conceived and honestly executed, we are all indebted to it. The movies have not undermined the influence of fiction. On the contrary, they have extended its field, carrying the ideas which are already current among readers to those too young, too impatient, or too uneducated to read.

So I make no apology for writing seriously about the problems of fiction writers; but until two years ago I should have felt apologetic about adding another volume to the writer's working library. During the period of my own apprenticeship—and, I confess, long after that apprenticeship should have been over—I read every book on the technique of fiction, the constructing of plots, the handling of characters, that I could lay my hands on. I sat at the feet of teachers of various schools: I have heard the writing of fiction analyzed by a neo-Freudian; I submitted myself to an enthusiast who saw in the glandular theory of personality determination an inexhaustible mine for writers in search of characters; I underwent instruction from one who drew diagrams and from another who started with a synopsis and slowly inflated it into a completed story. I have lived in a literary "colony" and talked to practicing writers who regarded their calling variously as a trade, a profession, and (rather sheepishly) as an art. In short, I have had firsthand experience with almost every current "approach" to the problems of writing, and my bookshelves overflow with the works of other instructors whom I have not seen in the flesh.

But two years ago—after still more years spent in reading for publishers, choosing the fiction for a magazine of national circulation, writing articles, stories, reviews and more extended criticism, conferring informally with editors and with authors of all ages about their work—I began, myself, to teach a class in fiction writing. Nothing was further from my mind, on the evening of my first lecture, than adding to the top-heavy literature on the subject. Although I had been considerably disappointed in most of the books I had read and all the classes I had attended, it was not until I joined the ranks of instructors that I realized the true basis of my discontent.

That basis of discontent was that the difficulties of the average student or amateur writer begin long before he has come to the place where he can benefit by technical instruction in story writing. He himself is in no position to suspect that truth. If he were able to discover for himself the reasons for his aridity the chances are that he would never be found enrolled in any class at all. But he only vaguely knows that successful writers have overcome the difficulties which seem almost insuperable to him; he believes that accepted authors have some magic, or at the very lowest, some trade secret, which, if he is alert and attentive, he may surprise. He suspects, further, that the teacher who offers his services knows that magic, and may drop a word about it which will prove an Open Sesame to him. In the hope of hearing it, or surprising it, he will sit doggedly through a series of instructions in story types and plot forming and technical problems which have no relation to his own dilemma. He will buy or borrow every book with "fiction" in the title; he will read any symposium by authors in which they tell their methods of work.

In almost every case he will be disappointed. In the opening lecture, within the first few pages of his book, within a sentence or two of his authors' symposium, he will be told rather shortly that "genius cannot be taught"; and there goes his hope glimmering. For whether he knows it or not, he is in search of the very thing that is denied him in that dismissive sentence. He may never presume to call the obscure impulse to set down his picture of the world in words by the name of "genius," he may never dare to bracket himself for a moment with the immortals of writing, but the disclaimer that genius cannot be taught, which most teachers and authors seem to feel must be stated as early and as abruptly as possible, is the death knell of his real hope. He had longed to hear that there was some magic about writing, and to be initiated into the brotherhood of authors.

This book, I believe, will be unique; for I think he is right. I think there is such a magic, and that it is teachable. This book is all about the writer's magic.

The Four Difficulties

So, having made my apologies, and stated my belief, I am going, from now on, to address myself solely to those who hope to write.

There is a sort of writer's magic. There is a procedure which many an author has come upon by happy accident or has worked out for himself which can, in part, be taught. To be ready to learn it you will have to go by a rather roundabout way, first considering the main difficulties which you will meet, then embarking on simple, but stringently self-enforced, exercises to overcome those difficulties. Last of all you must have the faith, or the curiosity, to take one odd piece of advice which will be unlike any of the exhortations that have come your way in classrooms or in textbooks.

In one other way, beside the admission that there is an initiate's knowledge in writing, I am going to depart from the usual procedure of those who offer handbooks for young authors. Open book after book devoted to the writer's problems: in nine cases out of ten you will find, well toward the front of the volume, some very gloomy paragraphs warning you that you may be no writer at all, that you probably lack taste, judgment, imagination, and every trace of the special abilities necessary to turn yourself from an aspirant into an artist, or even into a passable craftsman. You are likely to hear that your desire to write is perhaps only an infantile exhibitionism, or to be warned that because your friends think you a great writer (as if they ever did!) the world cannot be expected to share that fond opinion. And so on, most tiresomely. The reasons for this pessimism about young writers are dark to me. Books written for painters do not imply that the chances are that the reader can never be anything but a conceited dauber, nor do textbooks on engineering start out by warning the student that because he has been able to make a grasshopper out of two rubber bands and a matchstick he is not to think that he is likely ever to be an honor to his chosen profession.

Perhaps it is true that self-delusion most often takes the form of a belief that one can write; as to that I cannot say. My own experience has been that there is no field where one who is in earnest about learning to do good work can make such enormous strides in so short a time. So I am going to write this book for those who are fully in earnest, trusting to their good sense and their intelligence to see to it that they learn the elements of sentence and paragraph structure, that they already see that when they have chosen to write they have assumed an obligation toward their reader to write as well as they are able, that they will have taken (and are still taking) every opportunity to study the masters of English prose writing, and that they have set up an exigent standard for themselves which they work without intermission to attain.

It may be that it is only my extraordinary good fortune that I have met more writers of whom these things are true than deluded imbecile scribblers. But tragically enough I have met a number of sensitive young men and women who have very nearly been persuaded, because they had come up against one of the obstacles to writing which we are shortly going to consider, that they were unfit to write at all. Sometimes the desire to write overcame the humiliation they had had to undergo; but others dropped back into a life with no creative outlet, unhappy, thwarted, and restless. I hope this book persuades some who are hesitating on the verge of abandoning writing to make a different decision.

In my experience four difficulties have turned up again and again. I am consulted about them far oftener than I am asked for help in story structure or character delineation. I suspect that every teacher hears the same complaints, but that, being seldom a practicing author, he tends to dismiss them as out of his field, or to see in them evidence that the troubled student has not the true vocation. Yet it is the very pupils who are most obviously gifted who suffer from these disabilities, and the more sensitively organized they are the higher the hazard seems to them. Your embryo journalist or hack writer seldom asks for help of any sort; he is off after agents and editors while his more serious brother-in-arms is suffering the torments of the damned because of his insufficiencies. Yet instruction in writing is oftenest aimed at the oblivious tradesman of fiction, and the troubles of the artist are dismissed or overlooked.

The Difficulty of Writing at All

First there is the difficulty of writing at all. The full, abundant flow that must be established if the writer is to be heard from simply will not begin. The stupid conclusion that if he cannot write easily he has mistaken his career is sheer nonsense. There are a dozen reasons for the difficulty which should be canvassed before the teacher is entitled to say that he can see no signs of hope for this pupil.

It may be that the root of the trouble is youth and humility. Sometimes it is self-consciousness that stems the flow. Often it is the result of misapprehensions about writing, or it arises from an embarrassment of scruples: the beginner may be waiting for the divine fire of which he has heard to glow unmistakably, and may believe that it can only be lighted by a fortuitous spark from above. The particular point to be noted just here is that this difficulty is anterior to any problems about story structure or plot building, and that unless the writer can be helped past it there is very likely to be no need for technical instruction at all.

The "One-Book Author"

Second, and far more often than the layman would believe, there is the writer who has had an early success but is unable to repeat it. Here again there is a cant explanation which is offered whenever this difficulty is met: this type of writer, we are assured, is a "one-book author"; he has written a fragment of autobiography, has unburdened himself of his animus against his parents and his background, and, being relieved, cannot repeat his tour de force. But obviously he does not consider himself a one-book author, or we should hear nothing more from him. Moreover, all fiction is, in the sense used here, autobiographical, and yet there are fortunate authors who go on shaping, recombining, and objectifying the items of their experience into a long series of satisfactory books or stories. No; he is right in considering the sudden stoppage of his gift a morbid symptom, and right, usually, in thinking it can be relieved.

It is evident, if this writer had a deserved success, that he already knows something, presumably a great deal, of the technical end of his art. His trouble is not there, and, except by happy accident, no amount of counsel and advice about technique will break the deadlock. He is, in some ways, more fortunate than the beginner who cannot learn to write fluently, for at least he has given evidence of his ability to set down words in impressive order. But his first impatience at being unable to repeat his success can pass into discouragement and go on to actual despair; and an excellent author may be lost in consequence.

The Occasional Writer

The third difficulty is a sort of combination of the first two: there are writers who can, at wearisomely long intervals, write with great effectiveness. I have had a pupil whose output was one excellent short story each year —hardly enough to satisfy either body or spirit. The sterile periods were torture to her; the world, till she could write again, a desert waste. Each time she found herself unable to work she was certain she could never repeat her success, and, on first acquaintance, she very nearly persuaded me of it. But when the cycle was lived through from start to finish she always wrote again, and wrote well.

Here again no technical instruction can touch the difficulty. Those who suffer from these silences in which not one idea seems to arise, not one sentence to come irresistibly to the mind's surface, may write like artists and craftsmen when they have once broken the spell. The teacher-consultant must form a definite idea of the root of the trouble and give counsel accordingly. It may be, again, that some notion of waiting for the lightning of inspiration to strike is behind the matter. Often it is the result of such ideals of perfection as can hardly bear the light of day. Sometimes, but rarely, a kind of touchy vanity is at work, which will not risk any rebuff and so will not allow anything to be undertaken which is not assured in advance of acceptance.

The Uneven Writer

The fourth difficulty actually has a technical aspect: it is the inability to carry a story, vividly but imperfectly apprehended, to a successful conclusion. Writers who complain of this are often able to start a story well, but find it out of control after a few pages. Or they will write a good story so drily and sparely that all its virtues are lost. Occasionally they cannot motivate their central action adequately, and the story carries no conviction.

It is quite true that those who find themselves in this pass can be greatly helped by learning about structure, about the various forms which the story may take, of the innocuous "tricks of the trade" which will help a story over the stile. But even here the real difficulty has set in long before the story form is in question. The author has not the self-confidence necessary to present his idea well, or he is too inexperienced to know how his characters would act in real life, or he is too shy to write as fully and emotionally as he needs to write if his story is to come to life. The writer who turns out one weak, embarrassed, or abruptly told story after another obviously needs something more than to have his individual manuscripts criticized for him. As soon as possible he must learn to trust his own feeling for the story, and to relax in the telling, until he has learned to use the sure, deft stroke of the man who is master of his medium. So even this dilemma comes down, after all, to being a trouble in the writer's personality rather than a defect in his technical equipment.

The Difficulties Not in Technical Equipment

Those are the four difficulties oftenest met at the outset of an author's writing life. Almost everyone who buys books on fiction writing, or takes classes in the art of the short story, suffers from one or another of these troubles, and until they have been overcome he is able to get very little benefit from the technical training which will be so valuable to him later. Occasionally writers are stimulated enough by the classroom atmosphere to turn out stories during the course; but they stop writing the moment that stimulus is withdrawn. An astonishing number who really want ardently to write are unable even to do assigned themes, yet they turn up hopefully — sometimes year after year. Obviously they are looking for help that is not being given them; and obviously they are in earnest—ready to spend what time, effort, and money they can to emerge from the class of novices and "yearners" and take their place among productive artists.

What Writers Are Like

If these are the difficulties, then we must try to cure them where they arise — in the life and attitudes and habits, in the very character itself. After you have begun to see what it is to be a writer, after you learn how the artist functions and also learn to act in the same way, after you have arranged your affairs and your relations so that they help you instead of hinder you on your way toward the goal you have chosen, those books on your shelves on the technique of fiction, or those others which set up models of prose style and story structure for emulation, will look quite different to you, and be infinitely more helpful. This volume is not intended to replace those books on craftsmanship. There are some handbooks so valuable that no writer should be without them. In the appended bibliography I give the titles of those I have found most helpful for myself and for my pupils; I have no doubt that the list could be doubled or trebled to advantage. This book is not even a companion volume to such works as those; it is a preliminary to them. If it is successful it will teach the beginner not how to write, but how to be a writer; and that is quite another thing.

Cultivating a Writer's Temperament

First of all, then, becoming a writer is mainly a matter of cultivating a writer's temperament. Now the very word "temperament" is justly suspect among well-balanced persons, so I hasten to say that it is no part of the program to inculcate a wild-eyed bohemianism, or to set up moods and caprices as necessary accompaniments of the author's life. On the contrary; the moods and tempers, when they actually exist, are the symptoms of the artist's personality gone wrong — running off into waste effort and emotional exhaustion.

I say "when they actually exist," for much of the bumptious idiocy which the average man believes is an inalienable part of the artist's makeup has no being except in the eye of the beholder. He has heard tales of artists all his life, and very frequently he really believes "poetic license" to mean that the artist claims the right to ignore every moral code which inconveniences him. What the non-writer thinks about the artist would be of little account if it did not influence those who would like to write; they are persuaded against their will and their better sense that there is something fearful and dangerous in an artist's life, and some of the very shyness which we have seen as a mischief-maker comes from their giving too much credence to such popular notions.

False and Real Artists

After all, very few of us are born into homes where we see true examples of the artistic temperament, and since artists do certainly conduct their lives—necessarily—on a different pattern from the average man of business, it is very easy to misunderstand what he does and why he does it when we see it from the outside. The picture of the artist as a monster made up of one part vain child, one part suffering martyr, and one part boulevardier is a legacy to us from the last century, and a remarkably embarrassing inheritance. There is an earlier and healthier idea of the artist than that, the idea of the genius as a man more versatile, more sympathetic, more studious than his fellows, more catholic in his tastes, less at the mercy of the ideas of the crowd.

The grain of truth in the fin de siècle notion, though, is this: the author of genius does keep till his last breath the spontaneity, the ready sensitiveness, of a child, the "innocence of eye" that means so much to the painter, the ability to respond freshly and quickly to new scenes, and to old scenes as though they were new; to see traits and characteristics as though each were new-minted from the hand of God instead of sorting them quickly into dusty categories and pigeonholing them without wonder or surprise; to feel situations so immediately and keenly that the word "trite" has hardly any meaning for him; and always to see "the correspondences between things" of which Aristotle spoke two thousand years ago. This freshness of response is vital to the author's talent.

The Two Sides of a Writer

But there is another element to his character, fully as important to his success. It is adult, discriminating, temperate, and just. It is the side of the artisan, the workman and the critic rather than the artist. It must work continually with and through the emotional and childlike side, or we have no work of art. If either element of the ar-tist's character gets too far out of hand the result will be bad work, or no work at all. The writer's first task is to get these two elements of his nature into balance, to combine their aspects into one integrated character. And the first step toward that happy result is to split them apart for consideration and training!

"Dissociation" Not Always Psychopathic

We have all read a great many Sunday "feature stories," magazine articles, and books of popularized psychology; so our first impulse is to shy violently away from the words "dissociation of personality." A dual personality, to the reader who has a number of half-digested notions about the constitution of the mind, is an unlucky fellow who should be in a psychopathic ward; or, at the happiest, a flighty, hysterical creature. Nevertheless, every author is a very fortunate sort of dual personality, and it is this very fact that makes him such a bewildering, tantalizing, irritating figure to the plain man of affairs who flatters himself that he, at least, is all of a piece. But there is no scandal and no danger in recognizing that you have more than one side to your character. The journals and letters of men of genius are full of admissions of their sense of being dual or multiple in their nature: there is always the workaday man who walks, and the genius who flies. The idea of the alter ego, the other self, or higher self, recurs wherever genius becomes conscious of its own processes, and we have testimony for it in age after age.

Everyday Examples of Dual Personality

Indeed, the dual character of the genius is almost a commonplace. As a matter of fact, it is a commonplace for all of us, to some extent. Everyone has had the experience of acting with a decision and neatness in an emergency which seem later to him to savor of the miraculous; this was the figure which Frederick W. H. Myers used to convey his idea of the activity of genius. Or there is the experience of the "second wind" that comes after long grinding effort, when suddenly fatigue seems to drop away and a new character to arise like a phoenix from the exhausted mind or body; and the work that went so haltingly begins to flow under the hand. There is the obscurer, but cognate, experience of having reached a decision, solved a problem, while we slept, and finding the decision good, the solution valid. All these everyday miracles bear a relation to genius. At such moments the conscious and the unconscious conspire together to bring about the maximum effect; they play into each other's hands, supporting, strengthening, and supplementing each other, so that the resulting action comes from the full, integral personality, bearing the authority of the undivided mind.

The man of genius is one who habitually (or very often, or very successfully) acts as his less gifted brothers only rarely do. He not only acts in an event, but he creates an event, leaving his record of the moment on paper, canvas, or in stone. As it were, he makes his own emergency and acts in it, and his willingness both to instigate and perform marks him off from his more inert, less courageous comrades.

Everyone who has seriously wanted to write has some hint of this. Often it is in the very moment of vision that the first difficulties arise. Embarkation on the career is easy enough; an inclination to reverie, a love of books, the early discovery that it is not too difficult to turn a phrase — to find any or all of these things in one's first adolescent consciousness is to believe that one has found the inevitable, and not too formidable, vocation.

The Slough of Despond

But then comes the dawning comprehension of all that a writer's life implies: not easy daydreaming, but hard work at turning the dream into reality without sacrificing all its glamour; not the passive following of someone else's story, but the finding and finishing of a story of one's own; not writing a few pages which will be judged for style or correctness alone, but the prospect of turning out paragraph after paragraph and page after page which will be read for style, content, and effectiveness. Nor is this by any means all the beginning writer foresees. He worries to think of his immaturity, and wonders how he ever dared to think he had a word worth saying. He gets as stagestruck at the thought of his unseen readers as any sapling actor. He discovers that when he is able to plan a story step by step, the fluency he needs to write it has flown out the window; or that when he lets himself go on a loose rein, suddenly the story is out of hand. He fears that he has a tendency to make his stories all alike, or paralyzes himself with the notion that he will never, when this story is finished, find another that he likes as well. He will begin to follow current reputations and harry himself because he has not this writer's humor or that one's ingenuity. He will find a hundred reasons to doubt himself and not one for self-confidence. He will suspect that those who encouraged him are too lenient, or too far from the market to know the standards of successful fiction. Or he will read the work of a real genius in words, and the discrepancy between that gift and his own will seem a chasm to swallow his hopes. In such a state, lightened now and again by moments when he feels his own gift alive and surging, he may stay for months or years.

Every writer goes through this period of despair. Without doubt many promising writers, and most of those who were never meant to write, turn back at this point and find a lifework less exacting. Others are able to find the other bank of their slough of despond, sometimes by inspiration, sometimes by sheer doggedness. Still others turn to books or counselors. But often they are unable to tell the source of their baffled discomfort; they may even assign the reasons for their feeling of fright to the wrong causes, and think that they miss effectiveness because they "cannot write dialogue," or "are no good at plots," or "make all the characters too stiff." When they have worked as intensively as possible to overcome the weakness, only to find that their difficulties continue, there comes another unofficial weeding-out. Some drop away from this group; still others persist, even though they have reached the stage of dumb discomfort where they no longer feel that they can diagnose their own cases.

No ordeal by discouragement which editors, teachers, and older writers can devise is going to kill off the survivor of this type. What he needs to realize first is that he tried to do too much at once, and next, that although he started going about his self-education step by step, he took the wrong steps. Most of the methods of training the conscious side of the writer — the craftsman and the critic in him — are actually hostile to the good of the unconscious, the artist's side; and the converse of this proposition is likewise true. But it is possible to train both sides of the character to work in harmony, and the first step in that education is to consider that you must teach yourself not as though you were one person, but two.

The Advantages of Duplicity

To see why training oneself to be a writer is a double task, let us go rapidly over the process of story formation.

The Process of Story Formation

Like any other art, creative writing is a function of the whole man. The unconscious must flow freely and richly, bringing at demand all the treasures of memory, all the emotions, incidents, scenes, intimations of character and relationship which it has stored away in its depths; the conscious mind must control, combine, and discriminate between these materials without hampering the unconscious flow. The unconscious will provide the writer with "types" of all kinds — typical characters, typical scenes, typical emotional responses; the conscious will have the task of deciding which of these are too personal, too purely idiosyncratic to be material for art, and which of them are universal enough to be useful. It may also be called upon to add intentionally those special traits which turn too universal a figure into an individual character, to undertake the humanizing of a type-form —a necessity if the fiction is to convey a sense of reality.

Each writer's unconscious will be found to have, if I may put it so, a type-story of its own: because of the individual's history, he will tend to see certain dilemmas as dramatic and overlook others entirely, as he will also have his own idea of the greatest possible happiness and personal good. Of course, it follows that each writer's stories will always bear a fundamental likeness to each other. This need not be seen as a threat of monotony, but the conscious mind must be enough aware of it to alter, recombine, introduce elements of surprise and freshness into each new story project.

Because of the tendency of the unconscious to see things in types, it is the unconscious, in the long run, which dictates the form of the story.

(But this will be taken up more fully later. All that needs pointing out here is that if this is so a great deal of instruction on plot making is a waste of time. Certain ingenuities can be suggested, the popular story of any given period can be isolated and studied, and formulas for its writing can be devised; but unless a given formula is already congenial to the student he will get little help by attempting to model his own work upon it.) At any rate, the story arises in the unconscious. It then appears, sometimes only vaguely prefigured, at other times astonishingly definite, in the consciousness. There it is scrutinized, pruned, altered, strengthened, made more spectacular or less melodramatic; and is returned into the unconscious for the final synthesis of its elements. After a period of intense activity—which, however, goes on at so deep a level that the author himself occasionally feels he has "forgotten" or "lost" his idea—it once again signals to the conscious that the work of synthesis has been done; and the actual writing of the story begins.

The "Born Writer"

In the genius, or the "born writer," we see this process taking place so smoothly and often so rapidly that even this over-compressed scheme seems to misrepresent the story's history. But the genius, you must remember, is the man who by some fortunate accident of temperament or education can put his unconscious completely at the service of his reasonable intention, whether or not he is aware that this is so. The proof of this statement will emerge later, for the process of making a writer is the process of teaching the novice to do by artifice what the born writer does spontaneously.

Unconscious and Conscious

The unconscious is shy, elusive, and unwieldy, but it is possible to learn to tap it at will, and even to direct it. The conscious mind is meddlesome, opinionated, and arrogant, but it can be made subservient to the inborn talent through training. By isolating as far as possible the functions of these two sides of the mind, even by considering them not merely as aspects of the same mind but as separate personalities, we can arrive at a kind of working metaphor, impossible to confuse with reality, but infinitely helpful in self-education.

The Two Persons of the Writer

So, for a period, while the conception is useful to you, think of yourself as two-persons-in-one. There will be a prosaic, everyday, practical person to bear the brunt of the day's encounters. It will have plenty of virtues to offset its stolidity; it must learn to be intelligently critical, detached, tolerant, while at the same time remembering that its first function is to provide suitable conditions for the artist-self. The other half of your dual nature may then be as sensitive, enthusiastic, and partisan as you like; only it will not drag those traits out into the workaday world. It distinctly will not be allowed, by the cherishing elderly side, to run the risk of being made miserable by trying to cope emotionally with situations which call only for reason, or of looking ludicrous to the un-indulgent observer.

The Transparent Barrier

The first advantage that will be gained by your innocent duplicity is that you will have erected a transparent barrier between you and the world, behind which you can grow into your artistic maturity at your own pace. The average person writes just too much and not quite enough to have any great opinion of an author's life. It is unfortunate, but the unimaginative citizen finds something exquisitely funny about the idea that one aspires to make a name and a living by any such process as "stringing words together." He finds it presumptuous when an acquaintance announces that he has elected to give the world his opinion in writing, and punishes the presumption by merciless teasing. If you feel called upon to correct this unimaginative attitude you will have opportunities enough to keep you busy for a lifetime, but you will not—unless you have an extraordinary amount of energy — have much strength left for writing. The same plain man reacts as impulsively and naively to the successful writer. He is awestruck in his presence, but he is also very uncomfortable. Nothing but witchcraft, he seems to believe, could have made another human being so wise in the ways of his kind. He will turn self-conscious, and act either un-typically or refuse to act at all; and if you alarm him you will find yourself barred from one source of your material. This is a low piece of advice to give, but I give it without apology: keep still about your intentions, or you will startle your quarry.

Keep Your Own Counsel

Then, too, the writer is at a disadvantage shared by no novice of the other arts. He does use the medium of ordinary conversation, of friendly letters and business letters, when he exercises his profession; and he has no impressive paraphernalia to impose respect on the layman. Now that everyone has his portable typewriter, not even that badge of his profession is left to the young writer. A musical instrument, canvas, clay, carry their own persuasiveness by seeming exotic to the uninitiated. Even a good singing voice does not issue from every throat. Until your name has been in print again and again you may get only teasing for your pains if you prematurely announce your allegiance to writing. At that, most young writers would benefit by taking a leaf from the practitioners of other arts; the violinist does not carry around his violin, the artist does not carry his palette and brushes, unless he is intending to use them, either privately or before a well-disposed audience. Give yourself the advantage of the same discretion, at least while you are finding your feet.

One excellent psychological reason for an author to keep his profession to himself is that if you confess so much you are likely to go further and talk of the things you mean to write. Now words are your medium, and effective use of them your profession; but your unconscious self (which is your wishful part) will not care whether the words you use are written down or talked to the world at large. If you are for the moment fortunate enough to have a responsive audience you often suffer for it later. You will have created your story and reaped your reward in approval or shocked disapproval; in either case you will have hit your mark. Afterward you will find yourself disinclined to go on with the laborious process of writing that story at full length; unconsciously you will consider it as already done, a twice-told tale. If you can conquer the disinclination to write you may still find that a slightly flat, uninterested note creeps in, in spite of you. So practice a wise taciturnity. When you have completed a fair first draft you can, if you like, offer it for criticism and advice; but to talk too early is a grave mistake.

There are other advantages in considering yourself a two-in-one character. It should not be your sensitive, temperamental self which bears the burden of your relations with the outside world of editors, teachers, or friends. Send your practical self out into the world to receive suggestions, criticisms, or rejections; by all means see to it that it is your prosaic self which reads rejection slips! Criticism and rejection are not personal insults, but your artistic component will not know that. It will quiver and wince and run to cover, and you will have trouble in luring it out again to observe and weave tales and find words for all the thousand shades of feeling that go to make up a story.

Your "Best Friend and Severest Critic"

For another thing, your writing self is an instinctive, emotional creature, and if you are not careful you will find yourself living the life that will give you the least annoyance and the greatest ease instead of a life that will continually feed and stimulate your talent. The "artistic temperament" is usually perfectly satisfied to exercise itself in reverie and amuse itself in solitude, and only once in a long while will the impulse to write rise spontaneously to the surface. If you leave it to the more sensitive side of your nature to set the conditions of work and living for you, you may find yourself at the end of your days with very little to show for the gift you were born with. A far better idea is to realize from the start that you are subject to certain caprices of action, and to study yourself objectively until you find which of your impulses are sound and which are likely to lead you into the bogs of inertia and silence. At first you will find it a great bore to be forever examining yourself for tendencies and habits; later you will find it second nature. Still later you will come to enjoy it rather too much, and the same critical attention will have to be given to the task of turning your scrutiny away from your own processes when your analysis has passed the stage where it bears beneficial fruits. In short, you will have to learn to be your own best friend and severest critic —mature, indulgent, stern and yielding by turns.

The Right Recreation

Observe, though, that you are to be your own best friend—not simply your stern and disciplinary elder. No one else will be in a position to discover for you what is best in the way of stimulation, amusement, and friends. Perhaps music (however little you know about music) may have the effect of starting up the obscure internal processes which send you to the typewriter. In that case it will be the task of your elder self to find and purvey music to you— and to see that you are not put on the defensive when you are questioned about your astonishing taste for symphony orchestras or Negro spirituals. You will find, too, that some friends are excellent for you as a writer who are worthless to you otherwise — and vice versa. Too stimulating a social life can be as hard on a budding talent as none at all. Only observation will show you the effect of any group or person on you as a writer. Seeing a dull soul whom you doggedly adore, or a brilliant friend who irritates you, may have to be treated as a very special form of indulgence, to be yielded to only rarely. If you feel, after an evening with the stolid friend, that the world is a dry and dusty place, or if you are exasperated to the point of speechlessness by your brilliant acquaintance, not the warmest emotion for them will justify your seeing much of them while you are trying to learn to write. You will have to find other acquaintances, persons who, for some mysterious reason, leave you full of energy, feed you with ideas, or, more obscurely still, have the effect of filling you with self-confidence and eagerness to write.

Friends and Books

If you are not fortunate enough to find them—well, you will discover fairish substitutes on library shelves, and occasionally in the strangest guises. I had a pupil who battened on medical case reports, and another who recorded that a few hours with a popular scientific monthly, which she could hardly understand in spite of its being insultingly elementary, induced in her such a feeling of being glutted with neat, hard little facts that she ran off to retrieve the balance by a debauch of imaginative writing. I know a popular author who abhors the works of John Galsworthy, but something in Galsworthy's rhythm starts up his own desire to write; he alleges that after a few pages of The Forsyte Saga he can hear an "internal hum" which soon turns into sentences and paragraphs; on the other hand, Wodehouse, whom he considers a past master of modern humorous writing, plunges him into such depths of despond about his own performance that he takes care not to read the latest Wodehouse book until he has finished whatever he has in hand. Watch for a while, and see which authors are your meat and which your poison.

When the actual writing is to be done, your elder self must stand aside, only murmuring a suggestion now and again on such matters as your tendency to use repetitions, or to suggest that you are being too verbose, or that the dialogue is getting out of hand. Later you will call on it to consider the completed draft, or section, and with its help you will alter the manuscript to get the best possible effects. But at the time of writing, nothing is more confusing than to have the alert, critical, overscrupulous rational faculty at the forefront of your mind. The tormenting doubts of one's own ability, the self-conscious muteness that drops like a pall over the best story ideas, come from consulting the judge in oneself at the moment when it is the storyteller's turn to be in the ascendant. It is not easy at first to inhibit the running verdicts on every sentence, almost every word, that is written, but once the flow of the story has well set in, the critical faculty will be content to wait its turn.

The Arrogant Intellect

There is no arrogance like that of the intellect, and one of the dangers, as we have said, of studying the technique of story writing too solemnly is that the reason is confirmed in its delusion of being the more important member of the writing team. It is not. Its duties are indispensable but secondary; they come before and after the period of intensive writing. You will find that if you cannot rein in your intellect during this period it will be forever offering pseudo-solutions to you, tampering with motives, making the characters "literary" (which is often to make them stereotyped and unnatural), or protesting that the story which seemed so promising when it first dawned in your consciousness is really trite or implausible.

The Two Selves Not at War

But now I am in danger of making it seem that these two halves of the writing personality are at war with each other, when it is the exact contrary that is true. When each has found its place, when each is performing the functions which are proper to it, they play endlessly back and forth into each other's hands, strengthening, inciting, relieving each other in such a way that the resulting personality, the integral character, is made more balanced, mellow, energetic, and profound. It is precisely when they are at war that we get the unhappy artist—the artist who is working against the grain, or against his sober judgment, or, saddest of all, is unable to work. The most enviable writers are those who, quite often unanalytically and unconsciously, have realized that there are different facets to their nature and are able to live and work with now one, now another, in the ascendant.

The First Exercise

Now we come to the first exercise of a book which will be full of exercises. Its purpose is to show you how simple it is to see oneself objectively.

You are near a door. When you come to the end of this chapter put the book aside, get up, and go through that door. From the moment you stand on the threshold turn yourself into your own object of attention. What do you look like, standing there? How do you walk? What, if you knew nothing about yourself, could be gathered of you, your character, your background, your purpose just there at just that minute? If there are people in the room whom you must greet, how do you greet them? How do your attitudes to them vary? Do you give any overt sign that you are fonder of one, or more aware of one, than of the rest?

There is no deep, dark, esoteric purpose behind this exercise. It is a primer lesson in considering oneself objectively, and should be dismissed from your mind when you have learned what you can from it. Another time try sitting at ease and—using no gestures at all—tell yourself step by step how you comb your hair. (You will find it harder than you think.) Again, follow yourself at any small routine task. A little later take an episode of the day before; see yourself going up to it and coming away from it; and the episode itself as it might have looked to a stranger. At still another time think how you might have looked if you could follow yourself all day long from a little height. Use the fiction maker's eye on yourself to see how you would have appeared when you went in and out of houses, up streets and into stores, and back home at the end of the day.

Interlude: On Taking Advice

With the best of intentions, we usually go about the formation of a new habit or the eradication of an old one in the manner most calculated to defeat our purpose. Whenever you come across a piece of advice in these pages I exhort you not to straighten your spine, grit your teeth, clench your fists, and go at the experiments with the light of do-or-die on your countenance.

Save Your Energy

We customarily expend enough energy in carrying out any simple action to bring about a result three times greater than the one we have in view. This is true from the simplest matters to the most complex and of physical effort as well as mental. If we climb stairs, we climb them with every muscle and organ laboring as though our soul's salvation were to be found on the top step, and the result is that we grow resentful at the disproportionate returns we receive from our expended energy. Or, putting a great deal more energy out than we can use, we must take it up, somehow, in purposeless motion. Everyone has had the experience of pushing a door that looked closed with more vigor than was necessary and of falling into the next room as a consequence. Or we have picked up some light object which looked deceptively heavy. If you notice yourself on such an occasion, you will see that you must make a slight backward motion merely to retrieve your balance.

Imagination Versus Will in Changing Habits

In mental effort we are likely to go still more widely astray from some childish notion that it is laudable to exert that "slow, dead heave of the will" as often as possible. But in changing habits, you will find yourself getting your results far more quickly and with less "backwash" if you engage your imagination in the process instead of calling out the biggest gun of your character equipment first.

This is not a plea to abandon the will. There will be times and occasions when only the whole weight of the will brought to bear on the matter in hand will prove effective. But the imagination plays a far greater role in our lives than we customarily acknowledge, although any teacher can tell you how great an advocate the imagination is when a child is to be led into a changed course.

Displacing Old Habits

Old habits are strong and jealous. They will not be displaced easily if they get any warning that such plans are afoot; they will fight for their existence with subtlety and persuasiveness. If they are too radically attacked they will revenge themselves; you will find, after a day or two of extraordinarily virtuous effort, all sorts of reasons why the new method is not good for you, why you should alter it in line with this or that old habit, or actually abandon it entirely. In the end you will have had no good from the new advice; but you will almost certainly feel that you have given it a fair trial and that it has failed. Your mistake will have been that you tired yourself out and exhausted your good intentions before you had a chance to see whether or not the program was the right one for you.

This is a very simple but rather spectacular experiment which you can make that will teach you more about your own processes of putting an idea into operation than pages of exhortation and explanation. It is this:

A Demonstration

Draw a circle on a sheet of paper, using the bottom of a tumbler or something of that circumference as the guide; then make a cross through it. Tie a heavy ring or a key on a string about four inches long. Hold the end of the string with the ring hanging like the weight of a pendulum over the intersection of the cross, about an inch above the paper. Now think around the circle, following the circumference with your eyes and ignoring the ring and cord entirely.

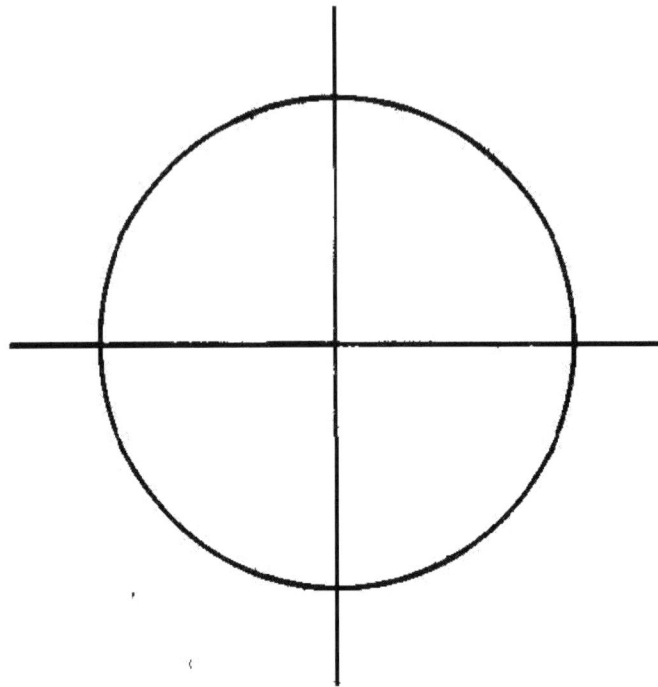

After a few moments the little pendulum will begin to swing around in the direction you have chosen, at first making a very small circle, but steadily widening out as it goes on. Then reverse the direction in thought only and follow the circle with your eyes in the other direction. . . . Now think up and down the perpendicular line; when that succeeds, shift to the horizontal. In each case the ring will stop for a moment and then begin to move in the direction of your thinking.

If you have not tried this experiment before you may feel that there is something uncanny about the result. There isn't. It is simply the neatest and easiest way of showing how important imagination can be in the sphere of action. Minute involuntary muscles take up the task for you. The will, you see, was hardly involved in the matter at all. And this, some French psychologists say, is the way to observe, in miniature, a "faith cure" in operation. At the least, it should demonstrate that it is not necessary to brace every nerve and muscle to bring about a change in your daily life.

The Right Frame of Mind

So, then, in doing the exercises in this book, turn yourself gently, in a relaxed and pleasant frame of mind, in the direction you want to go. See yourself, for a few minutes, doing the recommended experiment. After you have had a few successes by this method, you will find that it is capable of infinite extension. Consider that all the minor inconveniences and interruptions of habits are to the end of making a full and effective life for yourself. Forget or ignore for a while all the difficulties you have let yourself dwell upon too often; refuse to consider, in your period of training, the possibility of failure. You are not at this stage of your career in any position to estimate your chances justly. Things which look difficult or impossible to you now will be seen in truer perspective when you have gone a little further. Later you can take an inventory of yourself from time to time, see what is easy for you and what you do badly or imperfectly. You can consider then what steps to take to correct these definite faults, and by that time you will be able to work on yourself profitably, without discouragement or bravado.

Harnessing the Unconscious

To begin with, you must teach the unconscious to flow into the channel of writing. Psychologists will forgive us for speaking so airily about "teaching" the unconscious to do this or that. To all intents and purposes that is what happens; but less elegantly and more exactly we might say that the first step toward being a writer is to hitch your unconscious mind to your writing arm.

Wordless Daydreams

Most persons who are attracted by the idea of fiction at all are, or were in childhood, great dreamers. At almost any moment they can catch themselves, at some level, deep in reverie. Occasionally this reverie takes the form of recasting one's life, day by day or moment by moment, into a form somewhat nearer to the heart's desire: reconstructing conversations and arguments so that we come out with colors flying and epigrams falling around us like sparks, or imagining ourselves back in a simpler and happier period. Or adventure is coming toward us around the next corner, and we have already made up our minds as to the form it will take. All those naive and satisfying dreams of which we are the unashamed heroes or heroines are the very stuff of fiction, almost the materia prima of fiction. A little sophistication, a little experience, and we realize that we are not going to be allowed to carry off the honors in real life without a struggle; there are too many contenders for the role of leading lady or leading man. So, learning discretion and guile, we cast the matter a little differently; we objectify the ideal self that has caused us so much pleasure and write about him in the third person. And hundreds of our fellows, engaged secretly in just such daydreaming as our own, see themselves in our fictional characters and fall to reading when fatigue or disenchantment robs them of their ability to see themselves under any glamorous guise. (Not, thank heaven, that this is the only reason a book is ever read; but undoubtedly it is the commonest one.)

The little Brontes, with their kingdom of Gondaland, the infant Alcotts, young Robert Browning, and H. G. Wells all led an intensive dream-life which carried over into their maturity and took another form; and there are hundreds of authors who could tell the same stories of their youth. But there are probably thousands more who never grow up as writers. They are too self-conscious, too humble, or too solidly set in the habit of dreaming idly. After all, we begin our storytelling, usually, long before we are able to print simple words with infinite labor. It is little wonder that the glib unconscious should balk at the drudgery of committing its stories to writing.

Toward Effortless Writing

Writing calls on unused muscles and involves solitude and immobility. There is not much to be said for the recommendation, so often heard, to serve an apprenticeship to journalism if you intend to write fiction. But a journalist's career does teach two lessons which every writer needs to learn —that it is possible to write for long periods without fatigue, and that if one pushes on past the first weariness one finds a reservoir of unsuspected energy —one reaches the famous "second wind."

The typewriter has made the author's way more rocky than it was in the old days of quill and pen. However convenient the machine may be, there is no doubt about the muscular strain involved in typewriting; let any author tell you of rising stiff and aching from a long session. Moreover, there is the distraction set up by the little clatter of keys, and there is the strain of seeing the shafts continually dancing against the platen. But it is possible to make either typing or writing by hand second nature, so that muscular strain will not slow you down or keep you from writing.

So if you are to have the full benefit of the richness of the unconscious you must learn to write easily and smoothly when the unconscious is in the ascendant.

The best way to do this is to rise half an hour, or a full hour, earlier than you customarily rise. Just as soon as you can—and without talking, without reading the morning's paper, without picking up the book you laid aside the night before—begin to write.

Write anything that comes into your head: last night's dream, if you are able to remember it; the activities of the day before; a conversation, real or imaginary; an examination of conscience. Write any sort of early morning reverie, rapidly and uncritically. The excellence or ultimate worth of what you write is of no importance yet. As a matter of fact, you will find more value in this material than you expect, but your primary purpose now is not to bring forth deathless words, but to write any words at all which are not pure nonsense.

To reiterate, what you are actually doing is training yourself, in the twilight zone between sleep and the full waking state, simply to write. It makes no difference to the success of this practice if your paragraphs are amorphous, the thought vague or extravagant, the ideas hazy. Forget that you have any critical faculty at all; realize that no one need ever see what you are writing unless you choose to show it. You may, if you can, write in a notebook, sitting up in bed. If you can teach yourself to use the typewriter in this period, so much the better. Write as long as you have free time, or until you feel that you have utterly written yourself out.

The next morning begin without rereading what you have already done. Remember: you are to write before you have read at all. The purpose of this injunction will become clear later. Now all you need to concern yourself with is the mere performance of the exercise.

Double Your "Output"

After a day or two you will find that there is a certain number of words that you can write easily and without strain. When you have found that limit, begin to push it ahead by a few sentences, then by a paragraph or two. A little later try to double it before you stop the morning's work.

Within a very short time you will find that the exercise has begun to bear fruit. The actual labor of writing no longer seems arduous or dull. You will have begun to feel that you can get as much (far more really) from a written reverie as from one that goes on almost wordlessly in the back of your mind. When you can wake, reach out for your pencil, and begin to write almost on one impulse, you will be ready for the next step. Keep the material you have written—under lock and key if that is the only way to save yourself from self-consciousness. It will have uses you can hardly foresee.

As you take up the next exercise, you can return, in this morning task, to the limit that seems easy and natural. (But you should be able to write more words than when you began.) Watch yourself carefully; if at any time you find you have slipped back into inactive reverie, it is time to exert pressure on yourself. Throughout your writing life, whenever you are in danger of the spiritual drought that comes to the most facile writer from time to time, put the pencil and paper back on your bedside table, and wake to write in the morning.

Writing on Schedule

At once, when you have put the suggestion in the last chapter into operation, you will find that you are more truly a writer than you ever were before. You will discover that now you have a tendency to cast the day's experiences into words, to foresee the use that you will make of an anecdote or episode that has come your way, to transform the rough material of life into fictional shape, more consistently than you did when writing was a sporadic, capricious occupation which broke out from time to time unaccountably, or was undertaken only when you felt that you had a story firmly within your grasp.

The moment you reach that stage, you are ready for the next step, which is to teach yourself to write at a given moment. The best way to do it is this:

Engaging to Write

After you have dressed, sit down for a moment by yourself and go over the day before you. Usually you can tell accurately enough what its demands and opportunities will be; roughly, at least, you can sketch out for yourself enough of your program to know when you will have a few moments to yourself. It need not be a very long time; fifteen minutes will do nicely, and there is almost no wage slave so driven that he cannot snatch a quarter of an hour from a busy day if he is in earnest about it. Decide for yourself when you will take that time for writing; for you are going to write in it. If your work falls off, let us say, after three-thirty in the afternoon, the fifteen minutes from four o'clock until quarter past four can safely be drafted as time of your own.

Well, then, at four o'clock you are going to write, come what may, and you are going to continue until the quarter-hour sounds. When you have made up your mind to that you are free to do whatever you like to do or must do.

A Debt of Honor

Now this is very important, and can hardly be emphasized too strongly: you have decided to write at four o'clock, and at four o'clock write you must! No excuses can be given. If at four o'clock you find yourself deep in conversation, you must excuse yourself and keep your engagement. Your agreement is a debt of honor, and must be scrupulously discharged; you have given yourself your word and there is no retracting it. If you must climb out over the heads of your friends at that hour, then be ruthless; another time you will find that you have taken some pains not to be caught in a dilemma of the sort. If to get the solitude that is necessary you must go into a washroom, go there, lean against the wall, and write. Write as you write in the morning —anything at all. Write sense or nonsense, limericks or blank verse; write what you think of your employer or your secretary or your teacher; write a story synopsis or a fragment of dialogue, or the description of someone you have recently noticed. However halting or perfunctory the writing is, write. If you must, you can write, "I am finding this exercise remarkably difficult," and say what you think are the reasons for the difficulty. Vary the complaint from day to day till it no longer represents the true state of affairs.

Extending the Exercise

For you are going to do this from day to day, but each time you are to choose a different hour. Try eleven o'clock, or a moment or two before or after lunch. Another time, promise yourself to write for fifteen minutes before you start for home in the evening; or fifteen minutes before you dine. The important thing is that at the moment, on the dot of the moment, you are to be writing, and that you teach yourself that no excuse of any nature can be offered when the moment comes.

While you are merely reading this recommendation you may be quite unable to see why it is put so emphatically. As you begin to put it into practice you will understand. There is a deep inner resistance to writing which is more likely to emerge at this point than in the earlier exercise. This will begin to "look like business" to the unconscious, and the unconscious does not like these rules and regulations until it is well broken in to them; it is incorrigibly lazy in its busy-ness and given to finding the easiest way of satisfying itself. It prefers to choose its own occasions and to emerge as it likes. You will find the most remarkable series of obstacles presented to you under the similitude of common sense: Surely it will be just as satisfactory to write from 4:05 to 4:20? If you break out of a circle you are likely to be cross

questioned, so why not wait till the circle breaks up by itself and then take your fifteen minutes? In the morning you could hardly foresee that you were going to work yourself into a headache that day; can work done under the handicap of a headache possibly be fit to do? And so on and on. But you must learn to disregard every loophole the wily unconscious points out to you. If you consistently, doggedly, refuse to be beguiled, you will have your reward. The unconscious will suddenly give in charmingly, and begin to write gracefully and well.

Succeed, or Stop Writing

Right here I should like to sound the solemnest word of warning that you will find in this book: If you fail repeatedly at this exercise, give up writing. Your resistance is actually greater than your desire to write, and you may as well find some other outlet for your energy early as late.

These two strange and arbitrary performances — early morning writing, and writing by prearrangement — should be kept up till you write fluently at will.

The First Survey

When you have succeeded in establishing these two habits — early morning writing and writing by agreement with yourself—you have come a long way on the writer's path. You have gained, on the one hand, fluency, and on the other control, even though in an elementary way. You know a great deal more about yourself, in all likelihood, than you did when you embarked on the exercises. For one thing, you know whether it was easier to teach yourself to write on and on, or whether writing by prearrangement seemed more natural. Perhaps for the first time you see that if you want to write you can write, and that no life is actually so busy as to offer no opportunities if you are alert to find them. Then, too, you should begin to think it less than miraculous that writers can bring out book after book, having found in yourself the same inexhaustible resources that issue in the work of others. The physical mechanism of writing should have ceased to be tiring and begun to take its place as a simple activity. Your realization of the writer's life is probably more vivid, and nearer to the truth, than it was before—which is in itself a long stride to have taken.

Now it is time to consider yourself and your problems objectively again; and if you have followed the exercises well you should have plenty of material for an illuminating first survey.

Reading Your Work Critically

Up to this point it is best to resist the temptation to reread your productions. While you are training yourself into facility in writing and teaching yourself to start writing whenever and wherever opportunity offers, the less you turn a critical eye upon your own material the better— even for a cursory survey. The excellence or triteness of your writing was not the matter under consideration. But now, turning back to see what it may reveal under a dispassionate survey, you may find those outpourings very enlightening.

The Pitfalls of Imitation

You will remember that one of the conditions set was that you should not have read one word before beginning the morning's task, nor, if at all possible, so much as spoken until you have finished. This is the reason. We all live so surrounded by words that it is difficult for us to discover, without long experience, what our own rhythms are, and what subjects do really appeal to us. Those who are sensitive enough to want ardently to become writers are usually a little too suggestible for their own good. Consciously or not, they may have fallen into the temptation of imitating an established author. It may be a genuine master of writing; it may be (and too often is) the author whose work is having the greatest vogue at the moment. No one who has not taught fiction writing can believe how often a pupil will say some such thing as, "Oh, I've just thought of the most marvelous Faulkner story!" or, more ambitiously, "I think I can make a regular Virginia Woolf out of it." The teacher who crassly says she would rather see a good story of the pupil's own is damned for a prig, or outspokenly argued with; for the notion that playing the sedulous ape to the extent of copying not only the prose style but the very philosophies and narrative forms of current popular authors seems to have been so inculcated in our apprentice writers that they genuinely believe they will become original authors by the process of imitation. The men and women who have served as their models, since they are writing from a strong native talent and according to their own personal tastes, grow, alter, change their styles and their "formulas," and the poor sedulous apes are left imitating the work of an outmoded period.

Discovering Your Strength

The best way to escape the temptation to imitate is to discover as early as possible one's own tastes and excellences. Here, in the sheaf of pages you have written during this period of habit-making, is priceless laboratory material for you. What, on the whole, do you write, when you set down the first things that occur to you? Try to read, now, as though you had the work of a stranger in your hands, and to discover there what the tastes and talents of this alien writer may be. Put aside every preconception about your work. Try to forget any ambitions or hopes or fears you may have entertained, and see what you would decide was the best field for this stranger if he were to consult you. The repetitions, the recurrent ideas, the frequent prose forms in these pages will give you your clues. They will show you where your native gift lies, whether or not you eventually decide to specialize in it. There is no reason to believe that you can write only one type of work, that you may not be fully as successful in some other line; but this examination will show you where your richest and most easily tapped vein lies.

In my experience, the pupil who sets down the night's dream, or recasts the day before into ideal form, who takes the morning hour to write a complete anecdote or a passage of sharp dialogue, is likely to be the short story writer in embryo. Certain types of character sketching, when it is brief and concerned with rather general (or even obvious) traits, point the same way. A subtler analysis of characters, a consideration of motives, acute self-examination (as distinct from romanticizing one's actions), the contrasting of different characters faced by the same dilemma, most often indicate the novelist. A kind of musing introspection or of speculation only sketched in is found in the essay writer's notebook, although with a grain of drama added, and with the particularizing of an abstract speculation by assigning the various elements of the problem to characters who act out the idea, there is promise of the more meditative type of novelist.

When this stage of instruction is reached there is often in my classes a burst of highly stimulating activity. Seeing the possibilities in the writing which they now feel came almost without effort, the pupils frequently branch into some type of work which they look on simply as recreation, and hammer away on their more difficult problems in their "working" time. These spontaneous manuscripts are usually very interesting, and often, with some shaping, can be turned into satisfactory finished work. They are a little rambling, a little discursive, but they have a fresh, unforced tone which is striking. About this time you will find that your work is already less patchy and uneven; you are striking your own stride and finding your own rhythm, as well as discovering which subjects have a perennial interest for you.

A Footnote for Teachers

Here I should like to add a footnote for other teachers, rather than for students of writing. I think that holding up the work of each pupil in class for the criticism of the others is a thoroughly pernicious practice, and it does not become harmless simply by allowing the manuscript to be read without assigning its authorship publicly.

The ordeal is too trying to be taken with equanimity, and a sensitive writer can be thrown out of his stride deplorably by it, whether or not the criticism is favorable. It is seldom that the criticism is favorable, when a beginner is judged by the jury of his peers. They seem to need to demonstrate that, although they are not yet writing quite perfectly themselves, they are able to see all the flaws in a story which is read to them, and they fall upon it tooth and fang. Until self-confidence arises naturally, and the pupil asks for group criticism, his work should be treated as utterly confidential by the teacher. Each will have his own rate of growth and it can only go on steadily if not endangered by the setbacks that come from embarrassment and self-consciousness. I recommend an almost inhuman taciturnity to my students, at least about work that is being done at the moment. There have been weeks when I have had nothing at all from the best workers in the class, only to have three or four full-length manuscripts from a single pupil at the end of the silent period. Beyond stipulating that each pupil must follow the exercises as they are given out, whether or not I see the material which is written from day to day, I assign no tasks.

The Critic at Work on Himself

Now, we will suppose, you have a kind of rough preliminary idea of yourself as a writer. It will be a very rough idea, still distorted by humility in some directions and overconfidence in others, but at least it will bear enough resemblance to your ultimate professional self to be worth working on. Even in this unfinished state you will realize that there are definite things which you can do for yourself that will improve the quality of your writing, provide you with occasions for writing, or stimulate you so that writing will follow naturally. It is time now to call on your prosaic side for the services it can render you. (As a matter of fact, it will already have been called on to read the material and find your self-revealed tastes, but that was only preliminary.) There are a hundred things it can do for you as soon as you have given it this much material to work on. If it is called in too soon, though, it hampers you more than it helps.

Here you are then, with all these pages and notebooks to be examined by your common sense, everyday character. By the cursory examination recommended in the last chapter you have already found the more obvious trends in your own work. Now it is time to be more specific, and to examine in detail what you have done. Your workaday self has been standing aside while you were about the business of teaching your unconscious to flow whenever you could find a moment for it; you will find now that it has been closely following the process, remarking your successes and failures, and getting ready with suggestions.

A Critical Dialogue

The next few paragraphs are much more naive and more outrageously dual than any dialogue you will ever have with yourself, but some such interchange as this between the sides of your nature should now take place:

"Do you know, I find that you write dialogue very well; you evidently have a good ear. But your passages of description aren't well done. They're stilted."

Here the culprit will probably murmur something about liking to write dialogue, but feeling silly when describing anything without the protection of quotation marks.

"Of course you love to write dialogue," you must return, "just because you do it well. But don't you realize that if you can't do straight passages and transitions smoothly you're going to get a jerky story? You'd better make up your mind, I should say, whether you want to write fiction or to specialize in playwriting. Either way, you've got a lot of work to do."

"Which should you say? That's almost as much in your department as mine?"

"Well, fiction, on the whole. You don't show much interest yet in dramatic and spectacular effects, or in building up to a visually effective climax. You unfold a character slowly and by means of dialogue. If you had all the time and paper in the world you could undoubtedly get to your point by using dialogue alone, but, you see, you have space and effectiveness to consider. You'll have to do some of it in straight narrative form. No, all in all, I think we'd better work on your weak spots. You might read a lot of E. M. Forster in your spare time. He gets from point to point remarkably well. In the meanwhile, here's a passage for you to meditate upon. It's from Edith Wharton's The Writing of Fiction:

'The use of dialogue in fiction seems to be one of the few things about which a fairly definite rule may be laid down. It should be reserved for the culminating moments, and regarded as the spray into which the great wave of narrative breaks in curving toward the watcher on the shore. This lifting and scattering of the wave, the coruscation of the spray, even the mere material sight of the page broken into short, uneven paragraphs, all help to reenforce the contrast between such climaxes and the smooth effaced gliding of the narrative intervals; and the contrast enhances that sense of the passage of time for the producing of which the writer has to depend on his intervening narration. Thus the sparing use of dialogue not only serves to emphasize the crises of a tale, but to give it as a whole a greater effect of continuous development.' "

Or the exhortation may take the form of remarking a minor stylistic matter, and you will address yourself on it: "By the way, do you realize that you overwork the word 'colorful'? Every time you're in too much of a hurry to find the exact word you want you fall back on that; you're using it to death. Very sloppy habit. In the first place it's, usually, too vaguely inclusive to give the effect you want, and in the second, it is being used by all the advertising writers in the country just now. Stay away from it for a while."

Be Specific in Suggestions

Although you may not be quite so direct as this in your discourse, still you are advised to address yourself directly on these points, making the complaints specific, and, wherever possible, suggesting specific remedies. You will remember more easily, and you will have re-enforced your own discontent with this or that element in your writing in such a way that you must take steps to correct the slipshod practice or confess that you are not working seriously at the profession you have chosen. Make a clean-cut issue for yourself wherever you are able to put your finger on a fault; if you suspect that there are weaknesses which you do not see for some reason, show your work to someone whose good taste and judgment you trust. You will often find that a reader who has no pretensions to literary knowledge can put a finger on your stylistic sins as directly as a writer, an editor, or a teacher; but turn to outside counsel only after you have done all you are able to do for yourself. In the long run, it is your taste and your judgment that must carry you over the pitfalls, and the sooner you educate yourself into being all things to your writing-character the better your prospects are.

Correction After Criticism

Press home all the points on which you have any doubts. Do you use too many short declarative sentences, or too many exclamation points? Is your vocabulary lush, or too severe? Are you so reticent that you slide over an emotional scene so rapidly that your reader may miss the very thing you are trying to convey? Do you indulge in blood-and-thunder past the point of credibility? Then try to find the antidote. The reticent writer can force himself to read Swinburne, or Carlyle, or any one of a number of contemporary authors who are more sensational than decorous. The over-sensational can reverse the recommendation, and read the eighteenth-century Englishmen, or such writers as William

Dean Howells, Willa Cather, Agnes Repplier. If you have a dull and prosy note, a course in the novels and stories of G.

K. Chesterton should be of advantage. There is almost no limit to the recommendations which could be made, but you must learn both to diagnose your own case and to find your own best medicine. When you have found your antidote, read with humility, determined to see the excellence in writers who are natively antipathetic to you; while you are performing your stylistic penance, give yourself no quarter. Leave the books which usually attract you severely alone.

The Conditions of Excellence

Next set yourself to discover if you can see any connection between a good morning's work and the conditions of the evening before. Can you tell whether or not the good writing came after you had spent an active day, or after a quiet one? Did you write more easily after going to bed early, or after a short sleep? Is there any observable connection between seeing certain friends and the vividness or dullness of the next morning's work? How did you write on the morning after you had been to a theater, or to an exhibition of pictures, or to a dance? Notice such things, and try to arrange for the type of activity which results in good work.

Dictating a Daily Regime

Then turn your attention to your daily regime. Most writers flourish greatly on a simple, healthy routine with occasional time off for gaiety. Here you will touch the very foundations of prosaic common sense, for you will have to decide on such matters as what diet suits you and what food you must leave alone. If you are going in for a lifetime of writing, it stands to reason that you must learn to work without the continual use of stimulants, so find what ones you can use in moderation and what must be dropped. Bursts of work are not what you are out to establish as your habit, but a good, steady, satisfying flow, rising occasionally to an extraordinary level of performance, but seldom falling below what you have discovered is your own normal output. A completely honest inventory, taken every two or three months, or twice a year at the least, will keep you up to the best and most abundant writing of which you are capable.

While you are having this honest showdown is the time to ask yourself whether you are allowing your temperamental side too much voice in the conduct of your daily life. Do you find yourself emotional and headstrong in situations where an unprejudiced observer would expect you to be dispassionate and judicial? Are you hampering yourself by being resentful or envious or easily depressed? These are all matters to be cleared up by quiet consideration. Envy, depression, resentment, will poison the very springs from which your work flows, and the sooner you eradicate the faintest traces of them the better your writing will be.

When you have these sessions, have them thoroughly. This close, analytical probing of yourself should be done rarely, but well. You must be not only strict with yourself but fair. A blanket condemnation will get you no further than uncritical self-approval. If there is a type of writing which you do well, by all means recognize it and encourage yourself by it. Hold your own good work up to yourself as a standard, and exact work of the same grade in other lines.

After each of these sessions you will see that you emerge with a clearer idea of yourself, your abilities, and your weaknesses. At first you are likely to emphasize some points over others, and later will be astonished at your own blindness to equally important items. But you will have learned how to keep a friendly, critical eye on your own progress, and what steps to take to bring yourself nearer your goal. Once more: don't follow yourself around, nagging and suggesting and complaining. When you feel that you would benefit by an inventory, set an hour for it, have it thoroughly, take the suggestions you have made; then come out and live without introspection till the next occasion for an overhauling arises.

Reading as a Writer

To get the most benefit from the corrective reading you are going to do after these periodical inventories, you must take a little trouble to learn to read as a writer. Anyone who is at all interested in authorship has some sense of every book as a specimen, and not merely as a means of amusement. But to read effectively it is necessary to learn to consider a book in the light of what it can teach you about the improvement of your own work.

Most would-be writers are bookworms, and many of them are fanatical about books and libraries. But there is often a deep distaste at the idea of dissecting a book, or reading it solely for style, or for construction, or to see how its author has handled his problems. Some feeling that one will never again get the bewitched, fascinated interest from any volume that one got as an uncritical but appreciative reader makes many a student-writer protest at the idea of putting his favorite authors under a microscope. As a matter of fact, when you have learned to read critically you will find that your pleasure is far deeper than it was when you read as an amateur; even a bad book becomes tolerable when you are engaged in probing it for the reasons for its stiff, unnatural effects.

Read Twice

At first you will find that the only way to read as a writer is to go over everything twice. Read the story, article, or novel to be studied rapidly and uncritically, as you did in the days when you had no responsibility to a book but to enjoy it. When you have finished put it aside for a while, and take up a pencil and scratch pad.

Summary Judgment and Detailed Analysis

First make a short written synopsis of what you have just read. Now pass a kind of summary judgment on it: you liked it, or didn't like it. You believed it, or were left incredulous. You liked part of it, and disliked the rest. (You may, if you like later, pass a moral judgment on it, too, but now confine your decisions to what you believe were the author's intentions, as far as you are able to discern them.)

Go on to enlarge on these flat statements. If you liked it, why did you? Don't be discouraged if your answer to this is vague at first. You are going to read the book again, and will have another chance to see whether you can find the source of your response. If part of it seemed good to you and the rest weak, see whether you are able to tell when the author lost your assent. Were the characters drawn with uniform skill, badly drawn, or inconsistent only occasionally? Do you know why you felt this?

Do any of the scenes stand out in your mind? Because they were well done, or because an opportunity was so stupidly missed? Remember any passage which arrested your attention for any reason. Is the dialogue natural, or, if stylized, is the formality purposeful or a sign of the author's limitations?

By this time you know some of your own weaknesses. How does the author you have just read handle situations which would be difficult for you?

The Second Reading

If it is a good book your list of questions should be long and searching, your answers particularized as much as possible. If it is not especially good it will be enough, at first, to find the weak spots in it and lay it aside. When you have made your synopsis and answered your own questions as far as possible, make a check against those you were not able to answer fully, or that seem to promise more enlightenment if you pursue them. Now start at the first word again, reading slowly and thoroughly, noting down your answers as they become plain to you. If you find any passage particularly well done, and especially if the author has used adroitly material which would be hard for you to handle, mark them. Later you can return to them and use them as models after further analysis.

You know now how the story ends; be on the watch for the clues to that ending which come early in the book or story. Where was the character trait that brings about the major complication first mentioned? Was it brought in smoothly and subtly, or lugged in by the ears? Do you find, on second reading, that there are false clues— passages which do not make the book more real, or which distort the author's intention, but which have been allowed to pass although they introduce an unnecessary element or actually mislead the reader? Go over such passages carefully, to make sure that you are not missing the author's full meaning, and be sure that you are right before concluding that the author was at fault.

Points of Importance

There is no end to the amount of stimulation and help you can get from reading with critical attention. Read with every faculty alert. Notice the rhythm of the book, and whether it is accelerated or slowed when the author wishes to be emphatic. Look for mannerisms and favorite words, and decide for yourself whether they are worth trying for practice or whether they are too plainly the author's own to reward you for learning their structure. How does he get the characters from one scene to another, or mark the passing of time? Does he alter his vocabulary and emphasis when he centers his attention first on one character and then on another? Does he seem to be omniscient, is he telling only what would be apparent to one character and allowing the story to dawn on the reader by following that character's enlightenment? Or does he write first from the viewpoint of one and then another, and then a third? How does he get contrast? Is it, for instance, by placing character against setting incongruously —as Mark Twain put his Connecticut Yankee down into the world of King Arthur's day?

Each writer will ask his own questions and find his own suggestive points. After the first few books—which you must read twice if you are to make good use of the work of others—you will find that you can read for enjoyment and for criticism simultaneously, reserving a second reading only for those pages where the author has been at his best or worst.

On Imitation

Now as to imitation for practice. When you have learned to find in the writing of others the material which is suggestive for your own work, you are in a position to imitate in the only way in which imitation can be of any use to you. The philosophies, the ideas, the dramatic notions of other writers of fiction should not be directly adopted. If you find them congenial, go back to the sources from which those authors originally drew their ideas, if you are able to find them. There study the primary sources and take any items over into your own work only when they have your deep acquiescence — never because the author in whose work you find them is temporarily successful, or because another can use them effectively. They are yours to use only when you have made them your own by full acquaintance and acceptance

Imitating Technical Excellences

But technical excellences can be imitated, and with great advantage. When you have found a passage, long or short, which seems to you far better than anything of the sort you are yet able to do, sit down to learn from it.

Study it even more closely than you have been studying your specimen book or specimen story as a whole. Tear it apart almost word by word. If possible, find a cognate passage in your own work to use for comparison. Let us assume, for instance, that you have trouble with that bugbear of most writers when they first begin to work seriously —conveying the passing of time. You either string out your story to no purpose, following your character through a number of unimportant or confusing activities to get him from one significant scene to another, or you drop him abruptly and take him up abruptly between two paragraphs. In the story you have been reading, which is about the length of the one you want to write, you find that the author has handled such transitions smoothly, writing just enough, but not a word too much, to convey the illusion of time's passing between two scenes. Well, then; how does he do it? He uses—how many words? Absurd as it may seem at first to think that anything can be learned by word-counting, you will soon realize that a good author has a just sense of proportion; he is artist enough to feel how much space should be given to take his character from the thick of action in one situation into the center of the next.

How to Spend Words

In a story of five thousand words, let us say, your author has given a hundred and fifty words to the passing of a night and a day, rather unimportant, in the life of his hero. And you? Three words, or a sentence perhaps: "The next day, Conrad, etc."* Something too skimpy about it altogether. Or, on the other hand, although there was nothing in Conrad's night and morning that was pertinent to the story in hand, and although you have already used up all the space you can afford in the sketching of your hero's character, by sheer inability to stop talking about him once you have started you may have given six hundred or a thousand words to the retailing of totally irrelevant matters about his day.

How does the author expend the words that you have counted? Does he drop for a few paragraphs into indirection, after having told the story up to this time straightforwardly? Does he choose words which convey action, in order to show that his hero, although not engaged during that time in anything that furthered the story, still has a full life while he is, as it were, offstage? What clues does he drop into the concluding sentence which allows him to revert to the true action? When you have found as much as you are able to find in that way, write a paragraph of your own, imitating your model sentence by sentence.

Counteracting Monotony

Again it may be that you feel that your writing is monotonous, that verb follows noun, and adverb follows verb, with a deadly sameness throughout your pages. You are struck by the variety, the pleasant diversity of sentence structures and rhythms in the author you are reading. Here is the real method of playing the sedulous ape: The first sentence has twelve words; you will write a twelve word sentence. It begins with two words of one syllable each, the third is a noun of two syllables, the fourth is an adjective of four syllables, the fifth an adjective of three, etc. Write one with words of the same number of syllables, noun for noun, adjective for adjective, verb for verb, being sure that the words carry their emphasis on the same syllables as those in the model. By choosing an author whose style is complementary to your own you can teach yourself a great deal about sentence formation and prose rhythm in this way. You will not wish, or need, to do it often, but to do it occasionally is remarkably helpful. You become aware of variation and tone in your reading, and learn as you read. Once having taken the trouble to analyze a sentence into its component parts and construct a similar one of your own, you will find that some part of your mind is thereafter awake to subtleties which you may have passed obliviously before.

Pick Up Fresh Words

Be on the alert to find appropriate words wherever you read, but before you use them be sure they are congruous when side by side with the words of your own vocabulary. Combing a thesaurus for what an old professor of mine used to call, contemptuously, "vivid verbs" will be far less useful than to find words in the midst of a living story; although a thesaurus is a good tool if it is used as it is meant to be.

Last of all, turn back to your own writing and read it with new eyes: read it as it will look if it makes its way into print. Are there changes you can make which will turn it into effective, diversified, vigorous prose?

Learning to See Again

The Blinders of Habit

The genius keeps all his days the vividness and intensity of
interest that a sensitive child feels in his expanding world. Many
of us keep this responsiveness well into adolescence; very few
mature men and women are fortunate enough to preserve it in
their routine lives. Most of us are only intermittently aware, even
in youth, and the occasions on which adults see and feel and hear
with every sense alert become rarer and rarer with the passage of
years. Too many of us allow ourselves to go about wrapped in our
personal problems, walking blindly through our days with our
attention all given to some petty matter of no particular
importance. The true neurotic may be engrossed in a problem so
deeply buried in his being that he could not tell you what it is that
he is contemplating, and the sign of his neurosis is his
ineffectiveness in the real world. The most normal of us allow
ourselves to become so insulated by habit that few things can
break through our preoccupations except truly spectacular events
— a catastrophe happening under our eyes, our indolent strolling
blocked by a triumphal parade; it must be a matter which
challenges us in spite of ourselves.

This dullness of apprehension to which we all submit spinelessly
is a real danger to a writer. Since we are not laying up for
ourselves daily observations, fresh sensations, new ideas, we tend
to turn back for our material to the same period in our lives, and
write and rewrite endlessly the sensations of our childhood or
early years.

Causes of Repetitiousness

Everyone knows an author who seems to have, somehow, only one
story to tell. The characters may be given different names from
book to book, they may be put into ostensibly different situations;
their story may end happily or on a tragic note. Nevertheless we
feel each time we read a new book by that author that we have
heard the same thing before. Whatever the heroine's name, we can
be sure that snowflakes will fall and melt on her eyelashes, or that

on a woodland walk her hair will be caught by a twig. A hero of D. H. Lawrence will drop into Lancashire dialect in moments of emotion, a heroine of Storm Jameson is likely to make a success at advertising writing and to have come from a shipbuilding family. Kathleen Norris will give you a blue mixing bowl in a sunny kitchen at least in every other book—and so on, ad infinitum. The temptation to rework material which has an emotional value for us is so great that it is almost never resisted; and there is no reason why it should be, if the reworking is well done. But often one is led to suspect that the episode is used through thoughtlessness and that with a little more trouble the author might have been able to turn up equivalent touches, just as valid, just as effective emotionally, and far less stale. The truth is that we all have a tendency to remember things which we saw under the clear, warm light of childhood, and to return to them whenever we wish to bring a scene to life. But if we continue to use the same episodes and items over and over we lose effectiveness.

Recapturing Innocence of Eye

It is perfectly possible to strip yourself of your preoccupations, to refuse to allow yourself to go about wrapped in a cloak of oblivion day and night, although it is more difficult than one might think to learn to turn one's attention outward again after years of immersion in one's own problems. Merely deciding that you will not be oblivious is hardly enough, although every writer should take the recommendation of Henry James, and register it like a vow: "Try to be one of the people on whom nothing is lost."* By way of getting to that desirable state, set yourself a short period each day when you will, by taking thought, recapture a childlike "innocence of eye." For half an hour each day transport yourself back to the state of wide-eyed interest that was yours at the age of five. Even though you feel a little self-conscious about doing something so deliberately that was once as unnoticed as breathing, you will still find that you are able to gather stores of new material in a short time. Don't plan to use the material at once, for you may get only the brittle, factual little items of the journalist if you do not wait for the unconscious mind to work its miracles of assimilation and accretion on them. But turn yourself into a stranger in your own streets.

A Stranger in the Streets

You know how vividly you see a strange town or a strange country when you first enter it. The huge red buses careening through London, on the wrong side of the road to every American that ever saw them — soon they are as easy to dodge and ignore as the green buses of New York, and as little wonderful as the drugstore window that you pass on your way to work each day. The drugstore window, though, the streetcar that carries you to work, the crowded subway, can look as strange as Xanadu if you refuse to take them for granted. As you get into your streetcar, or walk along a street, tell yourself that for fifteen minutes you will notice and tell yourself about every single thing that your eyes rest on. The streetcar: what color is it outside? (Not just green or red, here, but sage or olive green, scarlet or maroon.) Where is the entrance? Has it a conductor and motorman, or a motorman-conductor in one? What colors inside, the walls, the floor, the seats, the advertising posters? How do the seats face? Who is sitting opposite you? How are your neighbors dressed, how do they stand or sit, what are they reading, or are they sound asleep? What sounds are you hearing, what smells are reaching you, how does the strap feel under your hand, or the stuff of the coat that brushes past you? After a few moments you can drop your intense awareness, but plan to resume it again when the scene changes.

Another time speculate on the person opposite you. What did she come from, and where is she going? What can you guess about her from her face, her attitude, her clothes? What, do you imagine, is her home like?

It will be worth your while to walk on strange streets, to visit exhibitions, to hunt up a movie in a strange part of town in order to give yourself the experience of fresh seeing once or twice a week. But any moment of your life can be used, and the room that you spend most of your waking hours in is as good, or better, to practice responsiveness on as a new street. Try to see your home, your family, your friends, your school or office, with the same eyes that you use away from your own daily route. There are voices you have heard so often that you forget they have a timbre of their own; unless you are morbidly hypersensitive, the chances are that you hardly realize that your best friend has a tendency to use some words so frequently that if you were to write a sentence involving those words anyone who knew him would realize whom you were imitating.

All such easy and minor exercises are excellent for you if you really want to write. No one cares to follow a dull and stodgy mind through innumerable pages, and a mind is so easily freshened. Remember that part of the advice is to put what you notice into definite words before you abandon it to the manipulation of the unconscious. Finding the exact words is not always necessary, but much usable stuff will slip through your fingers if you do not emphasize it in this way. If you think, "Oh, I'm sure to remember that," you will find that you are often merely begging off from a hard task. You aren't finding the words for the new sensation simply because the words do not come easily; persistently going after the right phrase will reward you with a striking, well-realized item sometime when you need it badly.

The Rewards of Virtue

Shortly after you begin looking about you like this you will see that your morning's pages are fuller and better than before. It is not only that you are bringing new material to them every day, but you are stirring the latent memories in your mind. Each fresh fact starts a train of associations reaching down into the depths of your nature, releasing for your use sensations and experiences, old delights, old sorrows, days that have been overlaid in your memory, episodes which you had quite forgotten.

This is one reason for the inexhaustible resources of the true genius. Everything that ever happened to him is his to use. No experience is so deeply buried that he cannot revive it; he can find a type-episode for every situation that his imagination can present. By the simple means of refusing to let yourself fall into indifference and boredom, you can reach and revive for your writing every aspect of your life.

The Source of Originality

It is a commonplace that every writer must turn to himself to find most of his material; it is such a commonplace that a chapter on the subject is likely to be greeted with groans. Nevertheless it must be written, for only a thorough understanding of the point will clear away the misapprehensions as to what constitutes "originality."

The Elusive Quality

Every book, every editor, every teacher will tell you that the great key to success in authorship is originality. Beyond that they seldom go. Sometimes they will point out to the persistent inquirer someone whose work shows the "originality" that they require, and those free examples are often responsible for some of the direst mistakes that young writers fall into. "Be original, like William Faulkner," an editor will say, meaning only to enforce his advice by an instance; or "Look at Mrs. Buck; now if you could give me something like that—!" And the earnest inquirer, quite missing the point of the exhortation, goes home and tries with all his might to turn out what I have already complained of: "a marvelous Faulkner story," or "a perfect Pearl Buck novel." Once in a long while—a very long while, if my experience as editor and teacher counts for anything—the imitative writer actually finds in his model some quality so congenial that he is able to turn out an acceptable story on the same pattern. But for one who succeeds there are hundreds who fail. I could find it in my heart to wish that everyone who cut his coat by another man's pattern would find the result a crass failure. For originality does not lie down that road.

It is well to understand as early as possible in one's writing life that there is just one contribution which every one of us can make: we can give into the common pool of experience some comprehension of the world as it looks to each of us.

There is one sense in which everyone is unique. No one else was born of your parents, at just that time of just that country's history; no one underwent just your experiences, reached just your conclusions, or faces the world with the exact set of ideas that you must have. If you can come to such friendly terms with yourself that you are able and willing to say precisely what you think of any given situation or character, if you can tell a story as it can appear only to you of all the people on earth, you will inevitably have a piece of work which is original.

Now this, which seems so simple, is the very thing that the average writer cannot do. Partly because he has immersed himself in the writing of others since he was able to read at all, he is sadly apt to see the world through someone else's eyes. Occasionally, being imaginative and pliable, he does a very good job of it, and we have a story which is near enough to an original story to seem good, or not to show too plainly that it is derivative. But often those faults in comprehension, those sudden misunderstandings of one's own fictional characters, come from the fact that the author is not looking at the persons of his own creation with his own eyes; he is using the eyes of Mr. Faulkner, of Mr. Hemingway, of D. H. Lawrence or Mrs. Woolf.

Originality Not Imitation

The virtue of those writers is precisely that they have refused to do what their imitators do so humbly. Each of them has had a vision of the world and has set out to transcribe it, and their work has the forthrightness and vigor of all work that comes from the central core of the personality without deviation or distortion. There is always a faint flavor of humbug about a Dreiserian story written by some imitator of Mr. Dreiser, or one of those stark mystical Laurentian tales not directly fathered by D. H. Lawrence; but it is exceedingly hard to persuade the timid or hero-worshipping young writer that this must always be so.

The "Surprise Ending"

When the pitfall of imitation is safely skirted, one often finds that in the effort to be original an author has pulled and jerked and prodded his story into monstrous form. He will plant dynamite at its crisis, turn the conclusion inside out, betray a character by making him act uncharacteristically, all in the service of the God of Originals. His story may be all compact of horror, or, more rarely, good luck may conquer every obstacle hands down; and if the teacher or editor protests that the story has not been made credible, its author will murmur "Dracula" or "Kathleen Norris," and will be unconvinced if told that the minimum requirement for a good story has not been met: that he has not shown that he, the author, truly and consistently envisages a world in which such events could under any circumstances come to pass, as the authors whom he is imitating certainly do.

Honesty, the Source of Originality

So these stories fail from their own inconsistency, although the author has at his command, in the mere exercise of stringent honesty, the best source of consistency for his own work. If you can discover what you are like, if you can discover what you truly believe about most of the major matters of life, you will be able to write a story which is honest and original and unique. But those are very large "ifs," and it takes hard digging to get at the roots of one's own convictions.

Very often one finds a beginner who is unwilling to commit himself because he knows just enough about his own processes to be sure that his beliefs of today are not likely to be his beliefs of tomorrow. This operates to hold him under a sort of spell. He waits for final wisdom to arrive, and since it tarries he feels that he cannot commit himself in print. When this is a real difficulty, and not simply (as it sometimes is) a neurotic excuse to postpone writing indefinitely, you will find a writer who can turn out a sketch, a half-story with no commitments in it, but seldom more. Obviously what such a writer needs is to be made to realize that his case is not isolated; that we all continue to grow, and that in order to write at all we must write on the basis of our present beliefs. If you are unwilling to write from the honest, though perhaps far from final, point of view that represents your present state, you may come to your deathbed with your contribution to the world still unmade, and just as far from final conviction about the universe as you were at the age of twenty.

Trust Yourself

There are only so many dramatic situations in which man can find himself—three dozen, if one is to take seriously The Thirty-six

Dramatic Situations of Georges Polti—and it is not the putting of your character in the central position of a drama which has never been dreamed of before that will make your story irresistible. Even if it were possible to find such a situation it would be an almost heartbreaking feat to communicate it to your readers, who must find some recognizable quality in the story they read or be hopelessly at sea. How your hero meets his dilemma, what you think of the impasse—those are the things which make your story truly your own; and it is your own individual character, unmistakably showing through your work, which will lead you to success or failure. I would almost be willing to go so far as to say that there is no situation which is trite in itself; there are only dull, unimaginative, or uncommunicative authors. No dilemma in which a man can find himself will leave his fellows unmoved if it can be fully presented. There is, for instance, a recognizable thematic likeness between The Way of All Flesh, Clayhanger, and Of Human Bondage. Which of them is trite?

"Your Anger and My Anger"

Agnes Mure MacKenzie, in The Process of Litterature, says, "Your loving and my loving, your anger and my anger, are sufficiently alike for us to be able to call them by the same names: but in our experience and in that of any two people in the world, they will never be quite completely identical"; if that were not literally true there would be neither basis nor opportunity for art. And again, in a recent issue of the Atlantic Monthly, Mrs. Wharton, writing The Confessions of a Novelist, declares: "As a matter of fact, there are only two essential rules: one, that the novelist should deal only with what is within his reach, literally or figuratively (in most cases the two are synonymous), and the other that the value of a subject depends almost wholly on what the author sees in it, and how deeply he is able to see into it."

By returning to those quotations from time to time you may at last persuade yourself that it is your insight which gives the final worth to your writing, and that there is no triteness where there is a good, clear, honest mind at work.

One Story, Many Versions

Very early in my classes I set out to prove this by direct demonstration. I ask for synopses of stories reduced to the very bones of an outline. Of those that are offered I choose the "tritest." In one class this was offered: "A spoiled girl marries and nearly ruins her husband by her attitude toward money." I confess that when I read this aloud to my pupils my heart mis-gave me. I could foresee, myself, only one elaboration of it, with one possible variation which would only occur to those who could perform the rather sophisticated feat of "dissociation" upon it —those, that is, who could discover what their immediate response to the idea was, and then deliberately alter their first association into its opposite. The class was asked to write for ten minutes, expanding the sentence into a paragraph or two, as if they were going to write a story on the theme. The result, in a class of twelve members, was twelve versions so different from each other that any editor could have read them all on the same day without realizing that the point of departure was the same in each.

We had, to begin with, a girl who was spoiled because she was a golf champion, and who, since she was an amateur, nearly ruined her husband by traveling around to tournaments. We had a story of a politician's daughter who had entertained her father's possible supporters and who entertained her husband's employer too lavishly, leading him to think that his young right-hand man was too sure of promotion. We had a story of a girl who had been warned that young wives were usually too extravagant, and who consequently pinched and pared and cut corners till she wore out her husband's patience. Before the second variation was half-read the class was laughing outright. Each member realized that she, too, had seen the situation in some purely personal light, and that what seemed so inevitable to her was fresh and unforeseen to the others. I wish I could conclude this anecdote by saying that I never again heard one of them complain that the only idea she could think of was too platitudinous to use, but this story really happened.

Nevertheless it is true that not even twins will see the same story idea from the same angle. There will always be differences of emphasis, a choice of different factors to bring about the dilemma and different actions to solve it. If you can once believe this thoroughly you can release for your immediate use any idea which has enough emotional value to engage your attention at all. If you find yourself groping for a theme you may take this as a fair piece of advice, simple as it sounds: "You can write about anything which has been vivid enough to cause you to comment upon it." If a situation has caught your attention to that extent, it has meaning for you, and if you can find what that meaning is you have the basis for a story.

Your Inalienable Uniqueness

Every piece of writing which is not simply the purveying of straightforward information— as a recipe or a formula is, for example —is an essay in persuasion. You are persuading your reader, while you hold his attention, to see the world with your eyes, to agree with you that this is a stirring occasion, that that situation is essentially tragic, or that another is deeply humorous. All fiction is persuasive in this sense. The author's conviction underlies all imaginative representation of whatever grade.

Since this is so, it behooves you to know what you do believe of most of the major problems of life, and of those minor problems which you are going to use in your writing.

A Questionnaire

Here are a few questions for a self-exam-ination which may suggest others to you. It is by no means an exhaustive questionnaire, but by following down the other inquiries which occur to you as you consider these, you can come by a very fair idea of your working philosophy:

- *Do you believe in a God? Under what aspect? (Hardy's "President of the Immortals," Wells' "emerging God"?)*

- *Do you believe in free will or are you a determinist? (Although an artist-determinist is such a walking paradox that imagination staggers at the notion.)*

- *Do you like men? Women? Children?*

- *What do you think of marriage?*

- *Do you consider romantic love a delusion and a snare?*

- *Do you think the comment "It will all be the same in a hundred years" is profound, shallow, true or false?*

- *What is the greatest happiness you can imagine? The greatest disaster?*

And so on. If you find that you are balking at definite answers to the great questions, then you are not yet ready to write fiction which involves major issues. You must find subjects on which you are capable of making up your mind, to serve as the groundwork of your writing. The best books emerge from the strongest convictions — and for confirmation see any bookshelf.

The Writer's Recreation

Authors are more given than any other tribe to the taking of busmen's holidays. In their off-hours they can usually be found reading in a corner, or, if thwarted in that, with other writers, talking shop. A certain amount of shoptalk is valuable; too much of it is a drain. And too much reading is very bad indeed.

Busmen's Holidays

All of us, whether we follow writing as a career or not, are so habituated to words that we cannot escape them. If we are left alone long enough and forbidden to read, we will very soon be talking to ourselves—"sub-vocally" as the behaviorists say. This is the easiest thing in the world to prove: starve yourself for a few hours in a wordless void. Stay alone, and resist the temptation to take up any book, paper, or scrap of printed matter that you can find; also flee the temptation to telephone someone when the strain begins to make itself felt—for you will almost surely scheme internally to be reading or talking within a few minutes. In a very short while you will find that you are using words at a tremendous rate: planning to tell an acquaintance just what you think of him, examining your conscience and giving yourself advice, trying to recapture the words of a song, turning over the plot of a story; in fact, words have rushed in to fill the wordless vacuum.

Prisoners who never wrote a word in the days of their freedom will write on any paper they can lay hands on. Innumerable books have been begun by patients lying on hospital beds, sentenced to silence and refused reading; the last one to be reported was, I think, Margaret Ayer Barnes' Years of Grace, and long ago I remember reading that William Allen White's A Certain Rich Man came to him when he was "tossing pebbles into the sea" on an enforced vacation. A two year-old will tell himself stories, and a farmer will talk to a cow. Once we have learned to use words we must be forever using them.

Wordless Recreation

The conclusion should be plain. If you want to stimulate yourself into writing, amuse yourself in wordless ways. Instead of going to a theater, hear a symphony orchestra, or go by yourself to a museum; go alone for long walks, or ride by yourself on a bus-top. If you will conscientiously refuse to talk or read you will find yourself compensating for it to your great advantage.

One very well-known writer of my acquaintance sits for two hours a day on a park bench. He says that for years he used to lie on the grass of his back garden and stare at the sky, but some member of the family, seeing him so conveniently alone and aimless, always seized the occasion to come out and sit beside him for a nice talk. Sooner or later, he himself would begin to talk about the work he had in mind, and, to his astonishment, he discovered that the urgent desire to write the story disappeared as soon as he had got it thoroughly talked out. Now, with a purposeful air and in mysterious silence, he disappears daily, and can be found every afternoon (but fortunately seldom is) with his hands in his pockets staring at the pigeons in the park.

Another writer, almost tone-deaf, says that she can finish any story she starts if she can find a hall where a long symphony is being played. The lights, the music, her immobility, bring on a sort of artistic coma, and she emerges in a sleepwalking state which lasts till she reaches the typewriter.

Find Your Own Stimulus

Only experiment will show you what your own best recreation is; but books, the theater, and talking pictures should be very rarely indulged in when you have any piece of writing to finish. The better the book or the play is the more likely it is, not only to distract you, but actually to alter your mood, so that you return to your own writing with your attitude changed.

A Variety of Time-Fillers

Most established authors have some way of silent recreation. One found that horseback riding was the best relaxation for him; another, a woman, confessed that whenever she came to a difficult spot in a novel she was writing, she got up and played endless games of solitaire. (I believe it was Mrs. Norris, and I think she went so far as to say that she was not always certain to see an ace when she turned it up.) Another woman novelist found, during the war years, that she spun stories as fast as she knitted, and turned herself into a Penelope of the knitting needle, raveling a square of scarlet wool and starting on it again whenever she had a story "simmering." Fishing served a writer of detective stories, and another admits that he whittles aimlessly for hours. Still another said that she embroidered initials on everything she could lay her hands on.

Only an impassioned author could call some of these occupations by any name so glamorous as "recreation"; but it is to be noticed that successful writers, when talking about themselves as writers, say little about curling up in a corner with a good book. Much as they may love reading (and all authors would rather read than eat), they had all learned from long experience that it is the wordless occupation which sets their own minds busily at work.

The Practice Story

A Recapitulation

When you have succeeded for some weeks in rising early and writing, and in the second step of going off by yourself at a given moment and beginning to write, you are ready to combine the two; and you are within measurable distance of being ready for the key procedure which every successful artist knows. Why it is kept such a secret, and why it should take a different form in almost every writer, is a mystery. Perhaps because each worked it out for himself and so hardly realizes that it is a part of his special knowledge. But that is matter for another chapter. Now it is time to bring together the work of the conscious and unconscious in an elementary manner.

You were warned not to reread your own work before starting on each morning's writing. You were to try to tap the unconscious directly, not simply to call up from it by way of association a certain limited set of ideas; and, further, if you were to find your own stride it was necessary to free you from the hampering effects of having any example before your eyes. A newspaper, a novel, the speech of someone else, or even your own writing so long as you are under the influence of others—all have a circumscribing effect. We are very easily drawn into a circle of ideas; we fall into the rhythm of any book or newspaper we read.

The Contagiousness of Style

If you seriously doubt this, it is very easy to demonstrate how one can be caught up into the current of another's style. Choose any writer whose work has a strong rhythm, a decided personal style: Dickens, Thackeray, Kipling, Hemingway, Aldous Huxley, Mrs. Wharton, Wodehouse—anyone you like. Read your author until you feel a little fatigue, the first momentary flagging of attention. Put the book aside and write a few pages on any subject. Then compare those pages with the writing you have done in the early morning. You will find a definite difference between the two. You have insensibly altered your own emphasis and inflection in the direction of the author's in whom you have been engrossed.

Sometimes the similarity is so striking as to be almost ludicrous, although you intended no parody—may even have intended to write as independently as possible. We can leave it to the psychologists to discover that this is so, and to explain why it should be.

Find Your Own Style

The important matter is to find your own style, your own subjects, your own rhythm, so that every element in your nature can contribute to the work of making a writer of you. Study your own pages; among them you are to find some idea — preferably, this time, a fairly simple one — which offers you a good, obvious nucleus for a short story, an expanded anecdote (say, of The New Yorker's style), or a brief essay. Story material will be best. Anything that is there in your early morning work has real value for you. You will have something to say on the subject which is more than superficial comment. Abstract your idea from its too discursive setting and get down to the matter of considering it seriously.

The Story in Embryo

What shall you make of it? Remember, you are to look for a simple idea—something that can be finished in one sitting. Then, in that case, what will it need? Emphasis? Characters to embody in concrete form the speculations you have made in your sleepy state? Does it need to have certain factors made very plain, so that the conflict, whatever it is, runs no danger of seeming unimportant or of being overlooked? When you have decided what can and should be made of it, consider the details with care.

The Preparatory Period

Mind you, you are not yet to write it. The work you are doing on it is preliminary. For a day or two you are going to immerse yourself in these details; you are going to think about them consciously, turning if necessary to books of reference to fill in your facts. Then you are going to dream about it. You are going to think of the characters separately, then in combination. You are going to do everything you can for that story by using alternately your conscious intelligence and unconscious reverie on it. There will seem no end to the stuff that you can find to work over. What does the heroine look like? Was she an only child, or the eldest of seven? How was she educated? Does she work? Now perform the same labor on the hero, and on any secondary characters you need to bring the story to life. Then turn your attention to the scene, and to those background scenes in each character's life which you may never need to write of, but a knowledge of which will make your finished story that much more convincing.

When you have done everything you can in this way, say to yourself: "At ten o'clock on Wednesday I will begin to write it," and then dismiss it from your mind. Now and then it will rise to the surface. You need not reject it with violence, but reject it. You are not ready for it yet; let it subside again. Three days will do it no harm, will even help it. But when ten o'clock strikes on Wednesday you sit down to work.

Writing Confidently

Now; strike out at once. Just as you made yourself do the time exercises in the sixth chapter, take no excuses, refuse to feel any stage fright; simply start working. If a good first sentence does not come, leave a space for it and write it in later. Write as rapidly as possible, with as little attention to your own processes as you can give. Try to work lightly and quickly, beginning and ending each sentence with a good, clear stroke. Reread very little—only a sentence or two now and then to be sure you are on the true course.

In this way you can train yourself into good, workmanlike habits. The typewriter or the writing pad should not appear to you a good place to lose yourself in musing, or to work out matters you should have cleared up before. You may find it very helpful, before you begin to write, to settle on a first and last sentence for your story. Then you can use the first sentence as a springboard from which to dive into your work, and the last as a raft to swim toward.

A Finished Experiment

The exercise must end with a completed piece of work, no matter how long you labor at it. Later you will learn how to do writing which cannot be finished at a sitting; the best way is to make another engagement with yourself before you rise from the typewriter, and while the heat of work is still on you. You will find if you do this that you will come to meet yourself, as it were, in the same mood, and there will not be a noticeable alteration in the manner of your writing between one session and the next. But this story is to be finished on the day you begin it.

Whether or not you are going to like it when you read it later, whether or not you decide that you can do a better version of it if you try again, the exercise is not done properly unless you rise from the session with a complete practice story.

Time for Detachment

Put it away, and if your curiosity will let you, leave it alone for two or three days. At the very least let it stay unread overnight. Your judgment on it until you have slept is worth exactly nothing. One of two states of mind will interfere with any earlier appraisal. If you belong to one half the writing race, you will be worn and discouraged, and, reading your own story over with fatigue clouding every line, you will think it the dullest, most improbable, flattest tale ever told. Even if you reread it more favorably later when you are freshened by sleep and diversion, a memory of that first verdict is likely to cause you to wonder which of the judgments is right. And if the story is rejected by the first editor who sees it, you are likely to think that it is as bad as you feared, and you may refuse to give it another chance.

The other half of the brotherhood seems not to use up the last ounce of its energy in getting a story to its close. They, on reading their recent effort, will be still held by the impulse which set them writing in the first place. If they have fallen into errors of judgment, if they have been too verbose or compact, the same astigmatism that was responsible for the mistake in the first place will still operate to blind them to it.

You are simply not ready to read your story objectively when it is newly finished; and there are writers who cannot trust their objectivity toward their own work much under a month. So put it away and turn your attention to something else. Now is the time of times for the reading which you have been denying yourself. Your story is safely written, and will preserve the marks of your personality so tenaciously that not the deepest admiration for the work of another writer will be likely to endanger it. If even reading seems too great an effort, find some mild relaxation which takes your attention quite away from authorship. If you can make a definite break in your routine just here, so much the better. Some writers have an immediate impulse to begin work on another story; if you feel it, by all means give in to it. But if you feel that you never want to see paper and typewriter again, indulge yourself in that mood, too.

The Critical Reading

When you are refreshed, relaxed, and detached, take out your story and read it.

The chances are that you will find a great deal more in your manuscript than you are conscious of having put there. Something was at work for you while you wrote. Scenes which you thought absolutely vital to the proper telling of the story are not there at all; other scenes which you had not planned to write take their places. The characters have traits you had hardly realized. They have said things you had not thought of having them say. Here is a sentence cleverly emphasized which you had thought of as only a casual statement, but which needed that emphasis if the story was to be shapely. In short, you have written both less and more than you intended. Your conscious mind had less to do with it, your unconscious mind more, than you would have believed possible.

The Great Discovery

The Five-Finger Exercises of Writing

Now those are the five-finger exercises of writing. To recapitulate before we go further, for you can hardly hear too often these primary truths about your art, the writer (like every artist) is a dual personality. In him the unconscious flows freely. He has trained himself so that the physical effort of writing does not tire him out of all proportion to the effect he achieves. His intellect directs, criticizes, and discriminates wherever two possible courses present themselves, in such a way as to leave the more sensitive element of his nature free to bring forth its best fruit. He learns to use his intellect both cursively, as he works, and later, as he considers what he has done during the period of the creative flow. He replaces by conscious intention, and day by day, the drains made on his funds of images, sensations, and ideas, by keeping awake to new observations. Ideally, the two sides of his nature are at peace with each other and work in harmony; at the least he must be able to suppress one or the other at discretion. Each side of his character must learn to be able to trust the other to do what is in its field and to carry the full responsibility for its own work. He restrains each side of his mind to its own functions, never allowing the conscious to usurp the privilege of the unconscious, and vice versa.

Now we go a little more deeply into the contribution of the unconscious, and the piece of writing you have just finished is your laboratory specimen. If you have worked according to instructions, foreseeing as many of the points of your story as you were able to, if you thought and daydreamed about the story without beginning to write prematurely; if then when you had promised yourself to write you got straight to work without hesitation or apology, it is very nearly certain that the resulting piece of writing will be both shapelier and fuller than you could have expected. The story will be balanced in a way which seems more adroit than you would have believed possible. The characters will be more fully, more expertly drawn, and at the same time drawn with more economy, than if you had labored at them with all your conscious mind in action. In short, a faculty has been at work which so far we have hardly considered. The higher imagination, you may call it; your own endowment of genius, great or small; the creative aspect of your mind, which is lodged almost entirely in the unconscious.

The Root of Genius

For the root of genius is in the unconscious, not the conscious, mind. It is not by weighing, balancing, trimming, expanding with conscious intention, that an excellent piece of art is born. It takes its shape and has its origin outside the region of the conscious intellect. There is much that the conscious can do, but it cannot provide you with genius, or with the talent that is genius' second cousin.

Unconscious, Not Subconscious

But we are badly handicapped when we come to talk or write of it, for the mind is not yet fully explored. And there is an even more serious difficulty to be encountered. When the Freudian psychology first reached us, we began to hear, unfortunately for us, about the sub conscious. Freud himself has corrected that error in terminology, and it is the unconscious that is now mentioned in the canonical works. But for most of us, that unlucky "sub" carried a derogatory connotation, and we have not entirely freed ourselves from the idea that the unconscious is, in some way, a less laudable part of our makeup than our conscious mind. F.W.H. Myers, in his excellent chapter on "Genius" in Human Personality (which should be read by every prospective author), fell subject to the same temptation and spoke continually of the "subliminal uprush." Now the unconscious is not, in its entirety, either below or less than the conscious mind. It includes in its scope everything which is not in the forefront of our consciousness, and has a reach as far above our average intellect as it has depths below.

The Higher Imagination

This spatial terminology is also unfortunate. The thing to realize is that the unconscious must be trusted to bring you aid from a higher level than that on which you ordinarily function. Any art must draw on this higher content of the unconscious as well as on the memories and emotions stored away there. A sound and gifted person is one who draws on and uses continually these resources, who lives in peace and amity with all the reaches of his being; not one who suppresses, at the cost of infinite energy and vitality, every echo from the far region.

Come to Terms with the Unconscious

The unconscious should not be thought of as a limbo where vague, cloudy, and amorphous notions swim hazily about. There is every reason to believe, on the contrary, that it is the great home of form; that it is quicker to see types, patterns, purposes, than our intellect can ever be. Always, it is true, you must be on the watch lest a too heady exuberance sweep you away from a straight course; always you must direct and control the excess of material which the unconscious will offer. But if you are to write well you must come to terms with the enormous and powerful part of your nature which lies behind the threshold of immediate knowledge.

If you can learn to do this, you have less tiring, difficult labor to perform than you believed you had when you first turned to writing. There is a great field of technical knowledge which the writer can study, many shortcuts to effectiveness which can be learned by taking thought. Yet on the whole it is the unconscious which will decide on both the form and the matter of the work which you are planning, and which will, if you can learn to rely on it, give you a far better and more convincing result if you are not continually meddling with its processes and imposing on it your own notions of the plausible, the desirable, the persuasive, according to some formula which you have painstakingly extracted from a work on the technique of fiction, or laboriously plotted out for yourself from long study of stories in print.

The Artistic Coma and the Writer's Magic

The true genius may live his life long without ever realizing how he works. He will know only that there are times when he must, at all costs, have solitude; time to dream, to sit idle. Often he himself believes that his mind is empty. Sometimes we hear of gifted men who are on the verge of despair because they feel they are going through a "barren" period; but suddenly the time of silence is past, and they have reached the moment when they must write. That strange, aloof, detached period has been called "the artistic coma" by observers shrewd enough to see that the idleness is only a surface stillness. Something is at work, but so deeply and wordlessly that it hardly gives a sign of its activity till it is ready to externalize its vision. The necessity which the artist feels to indulge himself in solitude, in rambling leisure, in long speechless periods, is behind most of the charges of eccentricity and boorishness that are leveled at men of genius. If the period is recognized and allowed for, it need not have a disruptive effect. The artist will always be marked by occasional periods of detachment; the nameless faculty will always announce itself by an air of withdrawal and indifference, but it is possible to hasten the period somewhat, and to have it, to a limited extent, under one's control. To be able to induce at will the activity of that higher imagination, that intuition, that artistic level of the unconscious — that is where the artist's magic lies, and is his only true "secret."

The Third Person, Genius

The Writer Not Dual But Triple

So, almost insensibly, one arrives at the understanding that the writer's nature is not dual but triple. The third member of the partnership is—feeble or strong, constantly or spasmodically showing—one's individual endowment of genius. The flashes of insight, the penetrating intuitions, the imagination which combines and transmutes ordinary experience into "the illusion of a higher reality" — all these necessities of art, or, on a humbler level, all these necessities of any interpretation of life, come from a region beyond those we have been studying and learning to control. For most practical purposes it is enough to divide our minds roughly into conscious and unconscious; it is quite possible to live a lifetime (even the lifetime of an artist) without even so much comprehension of the mind's complexity. Yet by recognizing this third component of your nature, by understanding its importance to your writing, by learning to liberate it, to clear obstructions from its path so that it may flow unimpeded into your work, you perform the most vital service of which you are capable to yourself as a writer.

The Mysterious Faculty

Now you begin to see the basis of truth for that discouraging statement, "Genius cannot be taught." In a sense, of course, that is the literal truth; but the implications are almost entirely misleading. You cannot add one grain to this faculty by all your conscious efforts, but there is no reason why you should desire to. Its resources at the feeblest are fuller than you can ever exhaust. What we need is not to add to that natural endowment, but to learn to use it. The great men of every period and race—so great that we call them, for simplicity's sake, by the name of that one faculty alone, as though in them it existed with no admixture, the "geniuses" —are those who were able to free more of that faculty for use in their lives and in their works of art than the rest of mankind. No human being is so poor as to have no trace of genius; none so great that he comes within infinity of using his own inheritance to the full.

The average man fears, distrusts, ignores, or knows nothing of
that element of his nature. In moments of deep emotion, in
danger, in joy, occasionally when long sickness has quieted the
body and the mind, sometimes in a remote, dim apprehension
which we bring back with us from sleep, or from moments under
an anesthetic, everyone has intimations of it. Traces of it may be
seen at its most unmistakable and mysterious in the lives of the
prodigies of music* However mysterious and incomprehensible it
is, it exists; and it is no more "an infinite capacity for taking pains"
—as the old definition of genius would have it —than "inspiration
is perspiration"; a pure American delusion if ever there was one.
The process of transmitting one's intuitive knowledge, of
conveying one's insight at all satisfactorily, may be infinitely
laborious. Years may be spent finding the words to set forth the
illumination of a moment. But to confuse the labor with the genius
that instigated it is to be misled. When one learns to release this
faculty even inexpertly, or when it is released fortuitously, one
finds that so far from having to toil anxiously and painstakingly
for his effects one experiences, on the contrary, the miracle of
being carried along on the creative current.

Releasing Genius

Often the release does come accidentally. It is possible for an artist
to count on the energy from this region to carry out a book, story,
a picture, and yet never recognize it. He may even go so far as to
deny that any such thing as "genius" is in question. He will assure
you that, in his experience, it is all a matter of "getting into his
stride"; but what getting into his stride implies he may never
know, even though in that happy state he writes pages of clarity
and beauty beyond anything of which he is capable in his
pedestrian moments. Another may, in a burst of candor, tell you
that after mulling an idea over till his head aches he comes to a
kind of dead end: he can no longer think about his story or even
understand why it once appealed to him. Much later, when he is
least expecting it, the idea returns, mysteriously rounded and
completed, ready for transcribing. And so on. Most successful
writers arrive at their own method of releasing this faculty by a
trial-and-error process, so obscure that they can seldom offer a
beginner in search of the secret so much as a rule-of-thumb. Their
reports of their writing habits are so at variance with each other

that it is no wonder the young writer sometimes feels that his elders are all engaged in a conspiracy to delude and mislead him as to the actual process of literature.

Rhythm, Monotony, Silence

There is no conspiracy; there is, I should say, remarkably little jealousy or personal envy between writers. They will tell you what they can, but the more instinctively they are artists the less they are able to analyze their ways of working. What one finally gets, after long cross-questionings, after raking through reports, is no explanation, but usually simple statements of personal experience. They agree in reporting that the idea of a book or story is usually apprehended in a flash. At that moment many of the characters, many of the situations, the story's outcome, all may be —either dimly or vividly —prefigured. Then there is a period of intensive thinking and working over of the ideas. With some authors this is a period of great excitement; they seem intoxicated with the possibilities there before their minds. Later comes a quiescent period; and since almost every writer alive occupies himself in some quite idiosyncratic way in that interlude, it is seldom noticed that these occupations have a kind of common denominator. Horseback riding; knitting; shuffling and dealing cards; walking; whittling; you see they have a common denominator — of three figures, one might say. All these occupations are rhythmical, monotonous, and wordless. And that is our key.

In other words, every author, in some way which he has come on by luck or long search, puts himself into a very light state of hypnosis. The attention is held, but just held; there is no serious demand on it. Far behind the mind's surface, so deep that he is seldom aware (unless at last observation of himself has taught him) that any activity is going forward, his story is being fused and welded into an integrated work.

A Floor to Scrub

With no more clue than that you might be able to find some such occupation of your own; or you may recognize in some recurrent habit the promise of an occupation which would be useful to you. But the disadvantage of most of these accidentally discovered time-fillers is that they are only rude expedients. When they have been found they are seldom abandoned. Indeed, many writers reach a state of real superstition about the method which has worked for them. "I'd be all right if I had a floor to scrub," one of my pupils said to me, a professor's wife who had written in the intervals of bringing up a large family, and had found that her stories fell into line best when she was at work on the kitchen floor. A little success had brought her to the city to study; she convinced herself completely that she would be unable to write again till she got back to the rhythmical monotony of the scrubbing brush. This is an extreme case; but there are many famous authors with superstitions just as stubbornly and firmly, although less outspokenly, held as my middle-western housemother's. And indeed most of the methods which have been discovered accidentally are as arbitrary, wasteful, and haphazard as scrubbing floors.

There is a way to shorten that "incubating period" and produce a better piece of work. And that way is the writer's magic which you have been promised.

The Writer's Magic

X Is to Mind as Mind to Body

Let us pretend, for convenience, that this faculty, this genius which is present in all of us to a greater or less degree, has been isolated, analyzed, and studied; and found to stand in relation to the mind as the mind stands to the body. If the word "genius" is still too magniloquent a word for comfort, if you fear that under a wily guise you are being introduced to a spiritual quality which discomfits you, bear with the notions a little while, and call the faculty under consideration just ordinary X. Now X is to be thought of like a factor in an algebraic equation — X : Mind :: Mind : Body. In order to think intensively you hold your body still; at the most you engage it in some light, mechanical task which you can carry on like an automaton. To get X into action, then, you must quiet the mind.

This, you will observe, is exactly what those rhythmical, monotonous, wordless activities had as their obscure end: they were designed to hold mind as well as body in a kind of suspension while the higher, or deeper, faculty was at work. Insofar as they were successful, they were adopted and used over and over. But they are usually awkward, unsatisfactory, and not always uniform in their results. Moreover, they usually take far more time than the unknown quality needs to fulfill its functions. So, if you are fortunate enough to be a young writer who has not yet found a formula for that gestation period of the story, you are in a position to learn a quicker and better way to attain the same end.

Hold Your Mind Still

It is, in short, this: learn to hold your mind as still as your body.

For some this advice is so easy to take that they cannot believe anyone has difficulty in following it. If you belong to that happy group, do not try any of the more intensive exercises that follow. You do not need them, and they will only confuse you. But as you come to this spot in the book, close the book over your finger and shut your eyes, holding your mind, for only a few seconds, as still as you can.

Were you successful—even if for only a fraction of a moment? If you have never tried it before, you may be surprised and confounded to find how busy, fluttering, and restless your mind seems. "The chattering monkey," an Indian will say of his mind, half in scorn, half in indulgence; much as St. Francis of Assisi called his body, "My Brother, the Ass." "It skitters around like a water bug!" one experimenter exclaimed, in surprise. But it will stop skittering for you, after a little practice; at least it will be still enough to suit your purposes.

Practice in Control

The best practice is to repeat this procedure once a day for several days. Simply close your eyes with the idea of holding your mind quite steady, but feeling no urgency or tension about it. Once a day; don't push it or attempt to force it. As you begin to get results, make the period a little longer, but never strain at it.

If you discover that you cannot learn to do it so easily, try this way: Choose a simple object, like a child's gray rubber ball. (It is better not to select anything with a bright surface or a decided highlight.) Hold the ball in your hand and look at it, confining your attention to that one simple object, and calling your mind back to it quietly whenever it begins to wander. When you are able to think of the object and nothing else for some moments, take the next step. Close your eyes and go on looking at the ball, thinking of nothing else. Then see if you can let even that simple idea slip away.

The last method is to let your mind skitter all it pleases, watching it indulgently as it moves. Presently it will grow quieter. Don't hurry it. If it will not be entirely quiet, it will probably be still enough.

The Story Idea as the Object

When you have succeeded, even a little, try holding a story idea, or a character, in your mind, and letting your stillness center around that. Presently you will see the almost incredible results. Ideas which you held rather academically and unconvincingly will take on color and form; a character that was a puppet will move and breathe. Consciously or unconsciously every successful writer who ever lived calls on this faculty to put the breath of life into his creations.

Now you are ready to try the process in more extended form.

The Magic in Operation

Since this is practice work only (although more may come of the ideas you practice on than you expect) you may go at it rather mechanically. Choose any story idea at random. If you do not like to use one of your own cherished plots for this, here is a variation that will work as well: replace the character of a well-known book by someone you know in real life. If your sister had played the role of Becky Sharp, for example, what course would Vanity Fair have had to follow? Suppose Gulliver had been a woman? How vague, stiff, or incomplete the idea is, is of no importance. For our purposes, the less satisfactory it seems at the moment the more complete the demonstration of the method's effectiveness. Make a rough outline of the story. Decide on the main characters, then the secondary characters. See as plainly as possible what crucial situation you would like to put them into, and how you would like to leave them at the end. Don't worry about getting them either in or out of their dilemma; simply see them in it, and then see it resolved. Remember here the circle-and-ring experiment, and that envisaging the end was enough to set the means in motion.

Think over the whole story in a sort of pleasant, indulgent mood, correcting any obvious absurdities, reminding yourself of this or that item which you would like to include if it could be brought in naturally.

Now take that rough draft of a story out for a walk with you. You are going to walk till you are just mildly tired, and at that time you should be back at your starting place; gauge your distance by that. Get into a smooth and easy swing, not vigorous and athletic—a lazy, loafing walk is better at first, although it may become more rapid later. Now think about your story; let yourself be engrossed in it—but think of it as a story, not of how you are going to write it, or what means you will use to get this or that effect. Refuse to let yourself be diverted by anything outside. As you circle back to your starting place, think of the story's end, as though you were laying it aside after reading it.

Inducing the "Artistic Coma"

Now bathe, still thinking of it in a desultory way, and then go into a dim room. Lie down, flat on your back; the alternative position, to be chosen only if you find that the other makes you too drowsy, is to sit not quite fully relaxed in a low, large chair. When you have taken a comfortable position, do not move again: make your body quiet. Then quiet your mind. Lie there, not quite asleep, not quite awake.

After a while—it may be twenty minutes, it may be an hour, it may be two—you will feel a definite impulse to rise, a kind of surge of energy. Obey it at once; you will be in a slightly somnambulistic state indifferent to everything on earth except what you are about to write; dull to all the outer world but vividly alive to the world of your imagination. Get up and go to your paper or typewriter, and begin to write. The state you are in at that moment is the state an artist works in.

Valedictory

How good a piece of work emerges depends on you and your life: how sensitive, how discriminating you are, how closely your experience reflects the experience of your potential readers, how thoroughly you have taught yourself the elements of good prose writing, how good an ear you have for rhythm. But, limited or not, you will find, if you have followed the exercises, that you can bring forth a shapely, integrated piece of work by this method. It will have flaws, no doubt; but you will be able to see them objectively and work on eradicating them. By these exercises you have made yourself into a good instrument for the use of your own genius. You are flexible and sturdy, like a good tool. You know what it feels like to work as an artist.

Now read all the technical books on the writing of fiction that you can find. You are at last in a position to have them do you some good.

In Conclusion: Some Prosaic Pointers

Typewriting

As soon as you can, learn to typewrite. Then, if possible, learn to compose on the typewriter. Unless you write very rapidly and plainly, a first draft written by hand is usually one long waste motion. But be sure that you are sacrificing nothing in making the shift from handwriting to writing on a machine. There are persons who are never able to get the same qualities in the machine-written work which they can catch by the more leisurely method. Write two rather similar ideas, one by each method; compare the two. If the typewritten draft is more abrupt, if you find that ideas escape you there which are found in your handwritten draft, composing at the typewriter is not your proper method.

Have Two Typewriters

The professional writer should have two typewriters, a standard machine and a portable — preferably a noiseless portable. Choose machines with the same typeface; they should both be pica, or both be elite. This will enable you to write at your own convenience, in any room, at any free moment, or when traveling. And you can also leave an incompleted piece of work in the machine, as a mute reproach —if you find you need that.

Stationery

Raid a stationery store. There are innumerable pencils on the market, of all grades of softness and several colors. Try them all; you may find the ideal pencil for your purposes. A medium-soft lead is best for most writers: the pages do not smudge, yet no particular pressure is necessary when writing.

Try bond paper and "laid" paper —paper with a sleek, smooth finish. Many amateurs use a bond paper because they have never had the good fortune to find the smoother finish, yet the grain in a bond paper may irritate them like the feeling of painted china.

Try writing on loose paper, on pads of various sizes, and in notebooks. Have a notebook full of fresh sheets ready to take on any short journey. On a long journey carry typewriter paper and a portable machine, and make the most of your time.

Don't buy the heaviest and most impressive grade of bond paper for your finished manuscripts. It makes too bulky and heavy a package, and the paper shows wear more quickly than the less expensive grades. "A good sixteen-pound paper," is the way to ask for what you need. If the clerk doesn't understand you, find a better stationery store.

At the Typewriter: WRITE!

Teach yourself as soon as possible to work the moment you sit down to a machine, or settle yourself with pad and pencil. If you find yourself dreaming there, or biting your pencil end, get up and go to the farthest corner of the room. Stay there while you are getting up steam. When you have your first sentence ready, go back to your tools. If you steadily refuse to lose yourself in reverie at your worktable, you will be rewarded by finding that merely taking your seat there will be enough to make your writing flow.

If you are unable to finish a piece of work at one sitting, make an engagement with yourself to resume work before you rise from the table. You will find that this acts like a posthypnotic suggestion, in more ways than one. You will get back to the work without delay, and you will pick up the same note with little difficulty, so that your story will not show as many different styles as a patchwork quilt when it is done.

For Coffee Addicts

If you have an ingrained habit of putting off everything until after you have had your morning coffee, buy a thermos bottle and fill it at night. This will thwart your wily unconscious in the neatest fashion. You will have no excuse to postpone work while you wait for your stimulant.

Coffee Versus Maté

If you tend to drink a great deal of coffee when in the throes of composition, try replacing half of it by maté, a South American drink much like tea, but stimulating and innocuous. It can be bought at any large grocer's, and is very easy to prepare.

Reading

If you are writing a manuscript so long that the prospect of not reading at all until you have finished is too intolerable, be sure to choose books which are as unlike your own work as possible: read technical books, history, or, best of all, books in other languages.

Book and Magazine Buying

Have periodical debauches of book-buying and magazine-buying, and try to formulate to yourself the editor's possible requirements from the type of periodical he issues. Buy a good handbook on fiction markets, and whenever you find an editor asking for manuscripts which sound like the type you are interested in writing, send for a copy of the magazine if you cannot buy it nearer home.

Bibliography

Edith Wharton, The Writing of Fiction, Scribner, 1925.

A. Quiller-Couch, On the Art of Writing, Putnam, 1916.

A. Quiller-Couch, On the Art of Reading, Putnam, 1920.

Percy Lubbock, The Craft of Fiction, Scribner, 1921.

E. M. Forster, Aspects of the Novel, Harcourt, Brace, 1927.

The Novels of Henry James, Definitive Edition, Scribner, 1917. In particular, see Preface to The Ivory Tower.

Graham Wallas, The Art of Thought, Harcourt, Brace, 1926.

Mary Austin, Everyman's Genius, Bobbs Merrill, 1925.

Thomas Uzzell, Narrative Technique, Harcourt, Brace, 1923.

F.W.H. Myers, Human Personality and its Survival of Bodily Death, Longmans, Green, 1920. In particular, see the chapter on Genius.

Edith Wharton, "The Confessions of a Novelist." Atlantic Monthly, April, 1933. Percy Marks, The Craft of Writing, Harcourt, Brace, 1932.

S. T. Coleridge, Biographia Literaria. Various editions. Conversations of Eckermann with Goethe, tr. by John Oxenford, Dutton, 1931.

Longinus, On the Sublime, tr. by W. Rhys Roberts,

Macmillan, 1930. Alexander Pope, Essay on Criticism. Various editions.

William Archer, Play-Making, Dodd, Mead, 1912.

George Saintsbury, History of English Prose Rhythm, Macmillan, 1922.

Charles Williams, The English Poetic Mind, Oxford, 1932.

Anonymous, The Literary Spotlight, Doran. 24 English Authors, Mr. Fothergill's Plot, Oxford, 1931.

Douglas Bement, Weaving the Short Story, Richard R.

Smith, 1931. Ford Madox Ford, It Was the Nightingale, Lippincott, 1933.

Arnold Bennett, How to Live on 24 Hours a Day, Doran, 1910.

T. S. Eliot, Selected Essays, Harcourt, Brace, 1932.

Virginia Woolf, The Common Reader, Harcourt, Brace, 1925.

Virginia Woolf, Monday or Tuesday, Harcourt, Brace, 1921.

The Journals of Katherine Mansfield, edited by J. Middleton Murry, Knopf, 1927.

Storm Jameson, The Georgian Novel and Mr. Robinson, Morrow, 1929.

Blanche Colton Williams, Handbook on Story Writing, Dodd, Mead, 1930.

Henry Seidel Canby, Better Writing, Harcourt, Brace, 1926.

Paul Elmer More, The Shelburne Essays, 11 vols., Houghton Mifflin.

Irving Babbitt, The New Laokoon, Houghton Mifflin, 1910.

Lafcadio Hearn, Talks to Writers, Dodd, Mead, 1920.

And, finally, those who read French will treble the number of these books by the works of Sainte-Beuve, Remy de Gourmont, Gustave Flaubert, the Journals of the brothers Goncourt, Jules Lemaître, Paul Valéry, André Gide (see particularly Les Faux-Monnayeurs, or the excellent English translation, published in this country under the title The Counterfeiters, Knopf, 1927).

Resources

**Visit <u>Midwest Journal Press</u> for more material and
related books.**

http://dorotheabrandewakeupandlive.midwestjournalpress.com

Printed in Great Britain
by Amazon